WOK EVERY DAY

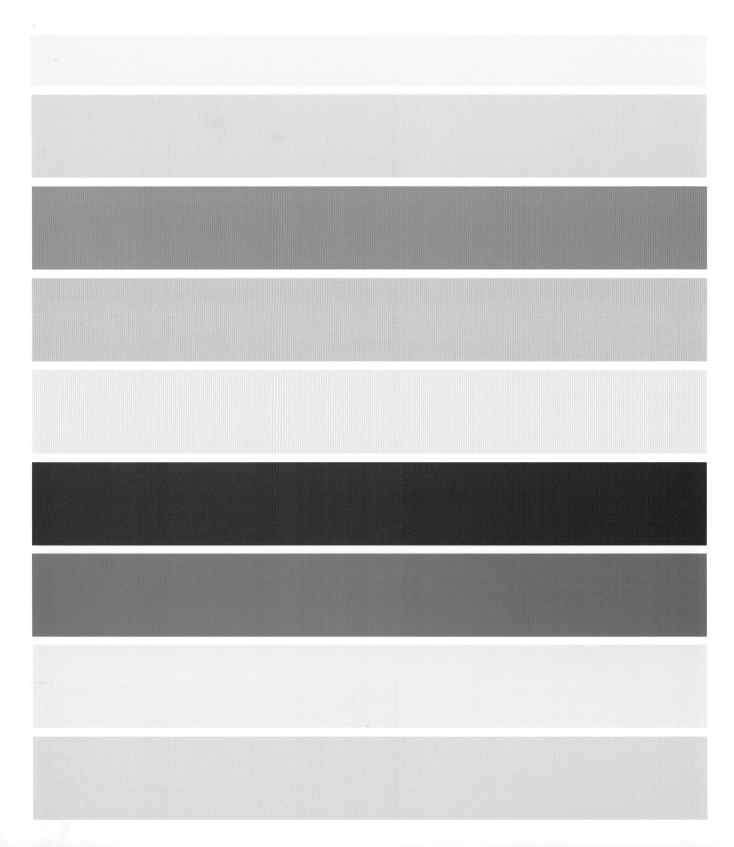

WOK EVERY DAY

FROM FISH & CHIPS TO CHOCOLATE CAKE —RECIPES AND
TECHNIQUES FOR STEAMING, GRILLING, DEEP-FRYING, SMOKING,
BRAISING, AND STIR-FRYING IN THE WORLD'S MOST VERSATILE PAN

BY BARBARA GRUNES AND VIRGINIA VAN VYNCKT

PHOTOGRAPHS BY SHERI GIBLIN

CHRONICLE BOOKS
SAN FRANCISCO

Library of Congress Cataloging-in-Publication Data:

Grunes, Barbara.

Wok Every Day / by Barbara Grunes and Virginia Van Vynckt;

photographs by Sheri Giblin. p. cm.

ISBN 0-8118-3195-7 (pbk.)

1. Wok cookery. I. Van Vynckt, Virginia. II. Title.

TX840.W65 .G78 2003

641.7'7—dc21

2002151401

Manufactured in Singapore

Designed by Paper Plane Studio

Food and prop styling by EK Food Productions: Erin Quon and Kim Konecny

Photographer's assistant: Guarina Lopez

Distributed in Canada by Raincoast Books

9050 Shaughnessy Street

Vancouver, British Columbia V6P 6E5

10 9 8 7 6 5 4 3 2 1

Chronicle Books LLC

85 Second Street

San Francisco, California 94105

www.chroniclebooks.com

ACKNOWLEDGMENTS

We would like to thank our agent, Martha Casselman,
for giving us a chance to do the book we've always wanted to do.
We're also grateful to our editors, Bill LeBlond and Amy Treadwell,
for helping us whip the concept and the book into shape,
and to copyeditor Kris Balloun for polishing our prose.

Alan Magiera and Vicki Cave tested and tasted recipes
and gave us much-appreciated suggestions on how to improve them.

We also thank all those cooks and guiding lights
through the years who helped us figure out how to put our woks
to the best use, especially Mai Leung.

DEDICATION

To Jerry, for all his help and kindness.
– Barbara Grunes

To Lian and Daniel, the ultimate wok kids,
And to Marv, for his constant support.
– Virginia Van Vynckt

CONTENTS

INTRODUCTION

ASK US WHICH PAN WE WOULD WANT IF WE WERE CAST AWAY ON A DESERT ISLAND, AND THERE'S NO QUESTION: *IT'S THE WOK.* BUILD A FIRE AND YOU CAN COOK ANYTHING IN A WOK. 🍜 AND WE DO MEAN ANYTHING, ANYWHERE. YEARS AGO, VIRGINIA WAS ON A HIKING TRIP IN THE HEART OF INDIA'S THAR DESERT—THE VERY DEFINITION OF THE MIDDLE OF NOWHERE—AND ENJOYED A SILKY, PERFECTLY COOKED CUSTARD, COMPLETE WITH CARAMELIZED SUGAR, FOR DESSERT. THE FRENCH-TRAINED EXPEDITION COOK HAD BURIED HIS WOK-LIKE PAN IN SAND HEATED BY THE WOOD FIRE TO SLOWLY BAKE HIS CRÈME CARAMEL. *NOW THAT'S COOKING.*

We don't expect that you'll embark on so chancy a venture, but you can use the wok for virtually every type of cooking method. Cooks in China and other Asian countries have been using woks and similar pans for millennia to stir-fry, deep-fry, steam, boil, poach, braise, and smoke foods. The wok's deep, rounded shape distributes heat well and makes it the ideal all-purpose pan.

When you have a wok, you can toss together a one-dish dinner for four in ten minutes or cook an elaborate banquet, from dumplings to dessert, using just one pan. You can quickly stir-fry broccoli or snow peas to tender-crispness. You can deep-fry oysters and vegetables into an irresistible tempura. You can steam a white chocolate bread pudding to die for. You can grill-wok mussels to smoky sweetness.

If your wok has been gathering dust or if you have never quite gotten around to buying one, now's the time to fire up that wonderful pan. After all, the single best way to season a wok is to simply use it as much as possible.

Wok Every Day explains in detail how to buy a wok, season it, care for it, and use it day in and day out for stir-frying, deep-frying, steaming, braising, poaching, boiling, smoking, and even grill cooking. It guides you through ingredients and basic preparation. You'll soon find yourself using your wok for all sorts of everyday and special-occasion meals, not just that twice-annual Chinese dinner.

In *Wok Every Day,* we naturally honor the pan's Chinese lineage. After all, *wok* is a Cantonese word, and stir-frying originated in China. But the book also celebrates the use of the wok or similar pans in kitchens throughout Asia, in places as far removed from one another as Korea and Myanmar (Burma). It also recognizes the enduring and increasing popularity of woks in the kitchens of North America and other regions in the West. The wok is just as suitable for frying chicken and cooking ravioli as it is for stir-frying beef and steaming dumplings.

So get out that wok and enjoy!

CHAPTER ONE

EQUIPMENT

CHOOSING AND CARING FOR YOUR WOK

BEFORE YOU CAN COOK IN A WOK, YOU HAVE TO BUY ONE. OR, IF YOU ALREADY OWN ONE THAT HAS BEEN GATHERING DUST, YOU NEED TO GET IT OUT OF THE CUPBOARD, CLEAN IT, RESEASON IT, IF NECESSARY, AND START USING IT. ⬙ TRUE, YOU CAN STIR-FRY IN A DEEP SKILLET (ALSO CALLED A SAUTÉ PAN), BUT IT REALLY IS NOT THE SAME. THE WOK'S DEEP, SLOPING SIDES MAKE IT A UNIQUE, ALL-PURPOSE PAN. MOST MANUFACTURERS OF ASIAN-STYLE COOKWARE USE THE TERMS "WOK" AND "STIR-FRY PAN" INTERCHANGEABLY. WE PREFER THE TERM "WOK" BECAUSE YOU CAN USE THIS MARVELOUS PAN FOR ALL SORTS OF COOKING METHODS OTHER THAN STIR-FRYING. ⬙ WHEN BUYING A WOK, YOU NEED TO DECIDE WHAT TYPE AND SHAPE TO GET— NOT AN EASY DECISION BECAUSE MANY KINDS OF WOKS AND SIMILAR PANS ARE AVAILABLE THESE DAYS. BASICALLY, YOUR DECISIONS BOIL DOWN TO THREE: WHETHER TO BUY A ROUND- OR FLAT-BOTTOMED WOK, WHAT SIZE OF PAN YOU NEED, AND WHAT MATERIALS IT SHOULD BE MADE OF.

ROUND OR FLAT?

If you want to stick with tradition, get the big bowl-shaped pan with two handles made of either plain metal or metal and wood. It's the only pan to use if you have a traditional Chinese stove: a wood- or coal-fired fireplace topped by a long shelf with holes cut into it. The wok's round bottom sits in the hole over the fire and gets blazingly hot—ideal for cooking foods in a small amount of oil or for creating a good deal of steam. Some professional-style home stoves sold in Western countries also have optional burners designed especially for woks. It's a nice addition if you use your wok frequently and can afford both the stove and the special burner.

However, the bowl-shaped wok does not transfer well to the flat gas or electric burners of Western-style stoves. That's why these woks come with a metal ring that sits atop the burner and holds the pan steady as you cook. This ring works fine on gas stoves, although electric stoves are a bit trickier. While the metal ring can be used successfully on electric burners, we prefer a flat-bottomed wok.

The traditional bowl-shaped wok is very deep, which allows you to control the cooking by pushing foods up the side to slow down their cooking and keeping them in the bottom of the pan for more intense heat. For example, if you've stir-fried a mixture of vegetables and chicken and want to thicken and reduce the sauce, just push the cooked ingredients up the sides of the wok, leaving the sauce in the bottom to bubble away. The depth of the traditional wok also makes it ideal for deep-frying, steaming, and boiling. The rounded bottom makes it especially easy to toss and stir foods as they cook.

The biggest disadvantage of the round-bottomed wok is that, even with the ring to hold it, the wok tends to rock and slide with vigorous stirring and tossing.

So why do we call it a wok? Wok is a Cantonese word that means "cauldron" or "pan." The term came into wide use in the United States because many of the early Chinese settlers in North America came from southern China. In Mandarin Chinese, the word for pan is guo.

Many of the woks sold for Western kitchens have the traditional deep, sloping sides, but their bottoms are flat, making them much more stable on gas and electric burners. Although some purists say it's not as easy to stir-fry foods in them as in round-bottomed woks, we think the difference is negligible. They are just as versatile as the traditional bowl-shaped woks and are ideal for most kitchens. Flat-bottomed woks often have one handle rather than two.

Some manufacturers make pans that are very similar to a wok but have somewhat shallower sides and a wider, flatter bottom. They're like a skillet crossed with a wok, and usually have one long handle, like a regular saucepan. These pans go by different names, including stir-fry pan, chef's pan, and *evasée,* the French name.

Because they're shallower than woks and often smaller, these pans are not as well suited for steaming and deep-frying, but work perfectly fine for stir-frying, braising, and poaching. Pay attention to size. Some hold only two quarts. That's fine if you're stir-frying for just yourself, but they're too small if you're cooking for two or more.

One newcomer to the wok market is the grill wok, which is set on the grill rack. Made of steel with a nonstick surface, it looks like a fairly deep skillet with holes punched in it. The holes let the intense heat from the coals sear the food as you stir-fry.

Although most Westerners associate the wok with Chinese cooking, the wok and its cousins are found throughout much of Asia. It is used on a daily or near-daily basis in Vietnam (where it's called chao, *the word for "fry"), Thailand, Cambodia, and Laos. In Singapore and the Philippines (where it's known as a* carajay), *it is used for Chinese-style dishes such as fried noodles. In Indonesia, Malaysia, and Singapore, a somewhat thicker pan is called a kuali. In India, the kadhai (or kerahi) is used for frying. In Myanmar (Burma), people cook in the* dare-oh, *a deep, rounded iron pan similar to a wok.*

LITTLE OR BIG?

Traditional woks are fourteen to sixteen inches in diameter, a good size for feeding large groups. We prefer larger woks because they're more adaptable. You can cook dinner for one or for eight with the same pan.

They are, however, a bit unwieldy to haul around and require a fair amount of storage space. Many cookware manufacturers sell woks or stir-fry pans that are ten, eleven, or twelve inches in diameter. Frankly, we think ten inches is a bit small for stir-frying; if the ingredients are crowded, they won't get hot enough and cook quickly. Perhaps even more important than diameter is depth. The pan should be deep enough so the chicken with black bean sauce doesn't fly around the stove.

We recommend a deep, twelve-inch-diameter wok at a minimum, and a fourteen-inch one if you have the space.

If you're really serious about wok cooking, you can buy a heavy carbon-steel wok as large as twenty-eight inches in diameter, like those huge woks you see in Chinese restaurants.

CARBON OR STAINLESS STEEL, IRON, OR ALUMINUM?

These days, woks and similar pans are available in the same materials that other pans are made of. But the traditional wok is usually constructed of cold rolled carbon steel. Purists believe that a wok should be made of carbon steel or maybe iron. Most woks in China are made of carbon steel because it is less expensive than other good heat-conducting metals, such as aluminum or copper.

Carbon-steel woks are inexpensive. You can usually buy a decent fourteen-inch carbon-steel wok, with tools and/or accessories, for under $50. Steel does require care, though—and the wok must be seasoned well and kept dry so it doesn't rust, become gummy, or latch onto foods. Once carbon steel is nicely seasoned, it turns black and stickproof, like a good cast-iron skillet.

In a carbon-steel pan, the heat tends to concentrate in the part of the pan closest to the flame, rather than dispersing throughout. That is not a bad trait in a wok. Because the bottom of the pan is very hot while the sides stay cooler, you have more control over the cooking.

Steel's biggest disadvantage is that, unless you cook in your wok everyday (a practice we highly recommend), it may never get truly seasoned, and the oil will tend to form a gummy, food-attracting surface on the inside of the pan. Another drawback is that many of the carbon-steel woks sold in this country are somewhat flimsy.

Carbon-steel woks also are not pretty. The average well-used wok looks like a reject from a garage sale. What woks lack in beauty, though, they make up for in functionality. And, despite all the choices available these days, our hearts still belong to those old, beat-up woks that have cooked so many of our meals and that carry so much tradition behind them.

Iron is another material traditionally used in Asia to make woks. Like carbon steel, it must be well seasoned and cared for. Cast iron holds heat exceptionally well, so it's perfect for wok-cooking on the grill and for bringing foods to the table and keeping them hot. Like carbon steel, cast iron is wonderful when well seasoned, not so wonderful when it's not, although you can buy iron woks with nonstick enameled coatings. Iron is very heavy, so unless you're looking for an inexpensive alternative to lifting weights at the health club, you may prefer not to wrestle a twelve- or fourteen-inch iron wok. Iron is also more expensive than steel.

Many of the woks sold in the West are made wholly or partly of aluminum, which is a superb heat conductor. It does tend to react with foods, especially acidic ones, and can pit and discolor. Anodized aluminum (the dark gray material that many higher-end pans are made of) has a special coating so it doesn't react with foods. Foods shouldn't stick too much to anodized aluminum as long as you get the pan very hot before adding ingredients.

Other woks are made of stainless steel with an aluminum bottom or, better yet, an aluminum core that runs up the pan between the layers of steel. (Because stainless steel is a lousy heat conductor, any pan made of this material must incorporate another metal.) Stainless-steel pans look good and don't react with most foods. They, too, need to be heated up well before adding ingredients.

Whatever material you choose, make sure the wok has some heft to it. A flimsy pan will burn your food, dent, and discolor in no time. Follow the same rule for woks that you do when buying other pans: The pan should look well made and feel heavy when you pick it up. You don't have to be quite as particular about the lid. Many wok lids are made of thin aluminum, no doubt to keep costs down. While a good, heavy, tight-fitting lid is nice, a thinner one will do the job.

Make sure the handles (or handle) are welded securely to the wok and don't wobble or feel flimsy. You don't want a handle to give way when you're lifting a wok full of food off the burner.

PLAIN OR NONSTICK?

Today, many woks have nonstick interiors. The advantages are that you can cook with less oil, the pan never has to be seasoned, foods don't stick, and cleanup is a breeze. While nonstick coatings have come a long way—you can even use metal utensils with many of the pans—there are disadvantages. A coated wok does not heat up as fast or as much, so foods sometimes steam rather than fry. And many of the coatings are designed to work best over medium to medium-high heat; very high heat may damage them. Even good nonstick coatings tend to eventually scratch, especially if you use metal utensils. This is mostly a cosmetic problem and does not necessarily ruin the pan.

Nonstick-coated woks do have two advantages over carbon-steel pans: They're better for cooking starchy foods such as fried rice or stir-fried noodles, which tend to stick to the interior of a regular wok, and they require less oil for cooking, making them ideal if you're concerned about fat intake.

If you buy a wok with a nonstick coating, make sure that both the wok and the coating are top quality. The best pans are heavy-gauge aluminum or steel with an aluminum core, and have several layers of a tough nonstick coating. The coating should come with a long warranty, preferably for the life of the pan.

An alternative to a nonstick wok is to buy a preseasoned one. This simply means the manufacturer has already seasoned the wok by firing it over intense heat. Preseasoned carbon-steel woks are blue rather than gray. Even a preseasoned wok needs a bit of breaking in to get that nice black-oil coating. And the interior will never be as completely nonstick as a commercially coated one.

STOVETOP OR ELECTRIC?

Electric woks are really just deep electric skillets. They do not get as hot as stovetop woks and, because the heating element is attached to the pan, it's more difficult to control the cooking. We much prefer the stovetop models.

However, if you're limited on stovetop space or if you intend to do a lot of tabletop cooking or serving, an electric wok may be just what you need.

A WOK FOR ALL SEASONS

YOUR MOTHER (OR GRANDMOTHER OR GREAT-GRANDMOTHER) PROBABLY HAD A CAST-IRON SKILLET. MAYBE YOU HAVE ONE, TOO. MAYBE YOU EVEN HAVE YOUR GRANDMA'S SKILLET, WITH ITS COAL-BLACK PATINA AND LOVELY ABILITY TO COOK ANY-THING WITHOUT STICKING. GRANDMA TOOK GOOD CARE OF IT, WAS CAREFUL NOT TO SCRUB IT WITH ABRASIVES, AND KEPT IT DRY AND OILED. SHE USED IT FOR EVERYTHING FROM FRIED CHICKEN TO PANCAKES.

Peanut oil, with its high smoking temperature and pleasant odor and flavor, is ideal for seasoning a wok. Corn and vegetable (soy) oils also are good choices. We suggest avoiding canola oil, which gives off a "fishy" odor and flavor as it burns, and safflower oil, which turns rancid easily.

Think of the wok as a bigger version of that iron skillet. The best way to season it is to use it often. As you keep cooking in a carbon-steel or cast-iron wok over high heat, the oil "burns" to the surface, gradually building up a protective black finish. A new wok is gray or bluish. A well-used one should be mostly black, inside and out.

If you buy a carbon-steel or cast-iron wok that is not preseasoned and does not have a nonstick coating, you will need to season it. The seasoning method you use depends on personal preference, on what coating is applied to the wok at the factory, and on the manufacturer's directions.

The first thing to do after bringing home a new wok is to get rid of the coating (usually machine oil, but occasionally lacquer) that was applied at the factory to keep the pan from rusting. Read the manufacturer's directions. If the wok has a lacquer coating, heat it over medium-high heat until it smokes. Let it cool, then wash it in soapy water, rinse in hot water, and put it on the stove over medium heat until it is completely dry. If the wok has an oil coating, you do not need to heat it before washing and drying it.

Once the pan is washed, you can use one of two seasoning methods:

Stovetop method: The most time-consuming but most effective method is one we learned from the Oriental Food Market and Cooking School in Chicago. It mimics what the manufacturers do when they preseason woks. First you "fire" the wok, then burn on the oil.

Set the wok directly on the burner over high heat, tilting and turning it as necessary, until the entire pan has turned blue. This may take a half hour or so. Then pour about a tablespoon of oil (peanut, vegetable, or corn oil is good) into the wok. Using a paper towel, rub the oil over the entire interior surface. Then heat the wok over medium heat for about 10 minutes, or until the pan starts to smoke a bit. Tilt the wok so the sides as well as the bottom blacken. As the oil burns, the wok's interior will begin to darken; use wadded-up paper towels to smear the oil evenly over the surface. Careful—the pan will be hot! Continue heating the wok and wiping the surface with oil until you no longer get black residue on the paper towel. Let the wok cool completely, then store it.

A less time-consuming variation of this method is to skip the initial step (firing the wok until it turns blue) and simply oil and heat it. You will need to repeat the oiling and heating process at least three times or until you no longer see a black residue on the paper towel. Let the wok cool completely, then store it.

Oven method: Be sure your wok has heatproof handles. Rub a tablespoon or two of oil over the interior of the wok and bake it in a 350°F oven for 1 hour. Once or twice during the baking, rub the oil in with a paper towel to evenly distribute it.

COMING CLEAN

Perhaps you've read that you should never use soap when cleaning a wok. Nonsense. Like any other pan, a wok needs to be cleaned of surface grime and any food bits that stick (and food will occasionally stick to even a well-seasoned wok).

It is true, though, that you should go light on the soap. Put a drop or two of dishwashing liquid in hot water, then lightly wash the wok with a dishcloth or plastic scrubber. Too much lather and too much scrubbing can remove some of the wok's protective oily coating. But if a touch of soap and water ruins the finish, the pan was not seasoned well to begin with. Just think of those old baking sheets you probably own that have turned brown with burned-on grease. It would take more than a touch of soap and a light scrubbing to rid them of their oil lacquer.

If the wok is plain carbon steel or cast iron, you will need to dry and oil it immediately after washing to keep it from rusting. Put it on the stove over medium-high heat. When the wok is completely dry, add about a teaspoon of vegetable oil and use a wadded-up paper towel to carefully rub the oil all over the inside of the pan. Let the wok heat for another few seconds, then take it off the heat. Let it cool completely, then store it.

We have seen suggestions that you rub oil on the outside of the pan as well, but we do not recommend this. The oil will create tons of smoke when you put the wok on the burner and could catch fire. A little rust on the outside of the pan may not look great, but it won't hurt anything.

There are three things you should never do with a carbon-steel wok (and many other woks as well):

Never clean a wok in the dishwasher. The corrosive detergent will harm the surface.

Don't use sharp metal utensils such as knives in a wok. They will damage the interior.

Never scrub a wok with abrasive cleaners or metal scrubbers. This will destroy that nice seasoned finish.

THE EXTRAS

Woks are pretty low-tech, and you don't need a raft of accessories or utensils to go with them. But there are a few basic tools worth having. You'll find more detailed information on each implement in the chapters on stir-frying, steaming, and so on.

BAMBOO STEAMER: Woven of strips of bamboo, this steamer includes a bottom compartment and a lid. The bottom part can be stacked with other steamers, and many steamers have two compartments, so you can steam two batches of food at once. Bamboo steamers are roomy, allow the steam to circulate freely, don't get too hot on the outside, and let water escape rather than drip back on the food. These baskets are often sold as part of a wok set, but they're also inexpensive to buy separately.

CLEAVER: This heavy-bladed knife makes quick work of chopping meats and dicing vegetables. If you stir-fry a lot, we recommend buying one. Although you can do many of the same chores with a good chef's knife, a cleaver is a wondrous tool and is essential for chopping through meat with the bone—for example, cutting the tips from chicken wings or cutting spareribs in half. (Of course, you may prefer to have the butcher where you buy your meats do this chore.)

COOKING CHOPSTICKS: Longer than eating chopsticks, these are used to stir and toss foods. You should own at least one pair for stir-frying noodles. Nothing works better than chopsticks for keeping the strands separate.

DEEP-FRYING/CANDY THERMOMETER: If you plan to use your wok for deep-frying, this thermometer is handy for getting an accurate reading of oil temperature.

DRAINING RACK: Most woks come with a semicircular metal rack that hooks onto the side of the pan. Also called a tempura rack, it's used for draining deep-fried foods.

SKIMMER/STRAINER: Often shaped like a flattened ladle, this tool is used to remove fried foods from the hot oil. The skimmers sold with woks often are made of brass, but any type of strainer will do.

STEAMER RACK: A round metal tray, some racks are wire grids, while others are solid aluminum or stainless steel with holes punched into them. The advantage is that it's roomy and does not absorb odors like a bamboo steamer. The disadvantage is that it gets very hot; trying to remove it immediately after steaming can be difficult.

WOK RING: If you have a round-bottomed wok, it should come with a ring. How you use this ring depends on the type of stove you have. On a gas burner, the wok sits on the narrower side of the ring to keep the pan elevated slightly above the flame. On an electric burner, the wok sits on the wider side of the ring, allowing the pan to rest directly on the heating element. If you lose the ring, you can buy a replacement for just a few dollars.

WOK SPATULA: This shovel-shaped utensil is a must-have for wok cooking. Its oblique handle and rounded spoon keep it from scratching the sides of the wok. If you have a nonstick-coated wok, you'll need to get a nylon or bamboo wok spatula, or use a regular flexible plastic spatula designed for nonstick pans.

IN EACH CHAPTER, WE
INCLUDE GUIDELINES FOR
SPECIFIC COOKING TECHNIQUES,
BUT HERE ARE A FEW GENERAL
WOK-COOKING TIPS TO KEEP IN MIND.

GENERAL COOKING TIPS

Asian cooking is traditionally 80 percent preparation and 20 percent cooking. This applies mostly to stir-frying but is also true of steaming and deep-frying. Except for braised dishes and some longer-steamed dishes, foods cook in the wok in mere minutes. All the ingredients must be ready to go once you heat up that pan.

Use care when cooking acidic foods, such as tomato sauce, in a wok. Especially if your wok is not completely "broken in," it's better to cook an acidic sauce in another pan, then toss it with the food just before serving. Or, use a wok with a nonstick coating. The acid can damage the oily black surface on a carbon-steel or iron wok's interior and give foods a metallic flavor.

Size matters. Whether you're deep-frying or stir-frying, cut foods into fairly small, uniform pieces so they cook quickly and evenly.

Be there. Whether you're stir-frying, deep-frying, or steaming, wok cooking requires hands- and eyes-on attention. Don't toss the food in the pan and walk away.

CHAPTER TWO

CROSS-CULTURAL DIM SUM

LITTLE DISHES WITH HEART

DIM SUM MEANS "A LITTLE BIT OF HEART" OR, MORE PRECISELY, "TOUCHING THE HEART LIGHTLY." IT GOT THAT NAME PRESUMABLY BECAUSE COOKS WHO LABOR OVER THESE LITTLE SNACKS WANT TO TOUCH THE HEARTS OF THEIR GUESTS. DESPITE ITS FANCIFUL ORIGINS, "DIM SUM" ACTUALLY HAS A MORE MUNDANE MEANING IN MODERN CHINESE: "SNACK."

The fried-everything appetizer plate of American chain restaurants is nonexistent in traditional Chinese cuisine. Dim sum is meant to be a feast for the palate—a little of this, a little of that. Something sour. Something sweet. Something crunchy. Something slippery. Something pungent. Something bland. It's a party in itself. If you eat in a restaurant in China or Taiwan, or in any of many Chinese restaurants around the world, you can revel in the culinary equivalent of heaven as you create your own meal from the carts of delectables, ranging from slippery rice noodles to crunchy wontons to sticky, chewy chicken wings (or feet, if you're in a really authentic Chinese restaurant). This complex interplay of flavors and textures is the key to a good dim sum.

The concept travels well. It's easy to put together a dim sum feast representing the flavors of various cultures. Like a patchwork quilt, the sum is even greater than its individually attractive parts.

Many dishes in this book make excellent party fare. Recipes in this chapter were specifically chosen for their interplay of flavors and textures, for how well they hold up (they can either be cooked ahead of time, or prepared well in advance and cooked quickly at the last minute), and for their portability. Select three or four or more to serve for a party, and we guarantee the harmony of flavors and textures will indeed touch your guests' hearts. Choose a couple of recipes that can be made in advance, and no more than one or two that need to be fried or steamed at the last minute.

A number of the dishes in this chapter are fried. Folks can talk about healthful eating all they like, but when it's party time, the crunchy, fried tidbits disappear the fastest. Of course, you don't want to serve only fried foods. Offer some steamed tidbits and maybe a salad or two for variety. To help you plan, we have included tips on making dishes in advance.

Accompany the food with a not-too-heavy beer, a light-style fruity wine such as a Riesling, or a light red with little tannin, such as a Beaujolais or Côtes du Rhône. For nonalcoholic beverages, we suggest fruit juices or a fruit-scented green tea, iced or hot.

SHRIMP SHAO MAI

You will find these delicate, open-faced pleated dumplings on dim sum carts in southern China and in Chinese restaurants around the world. For an attractive presentation, sprinkle the steamed dumplings with minced parsley or chopped hard-cooked egg and black sesame seeds. Or, before steaming, place a small shrimp on top of each dumpling, curving it around a green pea.

MAKES 24 DUMPLINGS

1 pound ground lean pork

1 cup peeled, deveined, and chopped raw small shrimp

1 tablespoon soy sauce

2 teaspoons dry white wine

¼ teaspoon salt

⅛ teaspoon freshly ground pepper

24 round dumpling wrappers, such as gyoza wrappers (see Note)

Chinese hot mustard or honey mustard for serving

In a mixing bowl, combine the pork, shrimp, soy sauce, wine, salt, and pepper.

To fill the dumplings, place a damp paper or kitchen towel over the wrappers to keep them from drying out. Place a wrapper on the wok surface, and put 1 to 1½ teaspoons of the filling in the center. Pull the sides up around the filling, pinching the wrapper into pleats and pressing it against the filling to form an open-faced dumpling. Tap the dumpling lightly to slightly flatten the bottom. Place the filled dumpling on an oiled plate. Repeat with the remaining wrappers and filling, using two plates to hold all the dumplings in a single layer.

Fill a wok one-half to two-thirds full of water and bring to a boil over high heat. Reduce the heat to medium and fit an oiled steamer rack or bamboo steamer in the wok. Arrange the dumplings in a single layer on the rack; if using a bamboo steamer, set one of the plates with the dumplings in the steamer. Cover and steam for 12 to 15 minutes, or until the wrappers are translucent and the filling is cooked through. You will need to either steam the dumplings in two batches, use two woks, or use a bamboo steamer with two compartments.

Remove the dumplings to a serving dish or serve them hot, right from the steamer, putting a plate underneath to catch drips. Accompany with mustard.

To make ahead of time: Assemble the dumplings and arrange them in a single layer on a wax paper–lined baking sheet. Cover the dumplings with a sheet of plastic wrap coated with nonstick cooking spray and refrigerate for up to 8 hours. Or, freeze them, uncovered, for about 1 hour, or until solid, then place them in plastic freezer bags. Seal and freeze for up to 1 month. Don't thaw them before cooking. Allow 2 to 3 minutes' extra steaming time.

Note: Store-bought dumpling wrappers tend to be a bit thicker and more "doughy" than homemade ones. But their convenience is worth the trade-off in texture. To enhance their translucence and melt-in-the-mouth tenderness, you can roll the wrappers a bit thinner with a heavy rolling pin.

STEAMED PORK AND GREEN BEAN DUMPLINGS

These dumplings are an adaptation of a recipe from Amy Chang, chef-owner of Yen King restaurant in Littleton, Colorado. She demonstrated how to make them at the annual Colorado Heritage Camp for Chinese-born adopted children, where the dumplings won the hearts of adults and children alike. Amy, in turn, learned to make them from her mother. The green beans are a tasty and unusual touch. Depending on the season, Amy and her mother sometimes use other vegetables, such as zucchini.

MAKES 48 TO 50 DUMPLINGS

3 dried shiitake mushrooms

½ ounce (½ bundle) bean threads

1 teaspoon plus 2 tablespoons soy sauce

½ teaspoon plus 2 tablespoons vegetable oil

2 tablespoons small dried shrimp, rinsed (see Note)

4 ounces green beans, finely sliced

¾ teaspoon salt

½ pound ground lean pork

1½ teaspoons sesame oil

1 teaspoon grated fresh ginger

1 package (10 ounces) round dumpling wrappers, such as gyoza wrappers (see Note)

Sweet Soy Dipping Sauce (page 204) for serving

Put the mushrooms in a heatproof bowl. Add hot water to cover and soak for 30 minutes, or until soft. Drain. Trim off and discard the stems. Finely chop the caps and set aside.

Put the bean threads in another heatproof bowl. Add hot water to cover and soak for 10 minutes, or until soft. Using scissors, snip the threads into ½- to 1-inch pieces. You should have about ⅓ cup.

Toss with the 1 teaspoon soy sauce and the ½ teaspoon vegetable oil. Set aside.

Put the shrimp in another heatproof bowl. Add hot water to cover and soak for 10 minutes. Drain and finely chop. Set aside.

While the mushrooms, bean threads, and shrimp are soaking, heat a wok over medium-high to high heat. Pour in the 2 tablespoons vegetable oil. Add the green beans and ¼ teaspoon of the salt. Stir-fry for 2 to 3 minutes, or until the beans are bright green. Transfer to a bowl and let cool.

In a medium bowl, combine the pork with the 2 tablespoons soy sauce and the sesame oil, ginger, and the remaining ½ teaspoon salt. Stir the mixture well. Add the chopped mushrooms, bean threads, dried shrimp, and green beans and stir well.

To fill the dumplings, have a small bowl of water near your work surface. Place a damp paper or kitchen towel over the wrappers to keep them from drying out. Place a wrapper on the work surface, and put 1 rounded teaspoon of the filling in the center. Dip your fingertip in the water and run it lightly around the edge of the wrapper. Fold the top of the wrapper over the filling and seal the dumpling, pleating the top edges as you go. Place the dumpling on an oiled plate. Repeat with the remaining wrappers and filling, using two or three plates to hold all the dumplings in a single layer.

Fill a wok one-half to two-thirds full of water and bring to a boil over high heat. Reduce the heat to medium and fit an oiled steamer rack or bamboo steamer in the wok. Arrange the dumplings in a single layer on the rack; if using a bamboo steamer, set one of the plates with the dumplings in the steamer. Cover and steam for about 15 minutes, or until the wrappers are tender and the filling is cooked through. You will need to either steam the dumplings in two batches, use two woks, or use a bamboo steamer with two compartments.

Serve hot with the dipping sauce.

To make ahead of time: Assemble the dumplings and arrange them in a single layer on a wax paper–lined baking sheet. Cover the dumplings with a sheet of plastic wrap coated with nonstick cooking spray and refrigerate for up to 8 hours. Or, freeze them, uncovered, for about 1 hour, or until solid, then place them in plastic freezer bags. Seal and freeze for up to 1 month. Don't thaw them before cooking. Allow 2 to 3 minutes' extra steaming time.

Note: If you can't find round dumpling wrappers, buy wonton wrappers and use a cookie cutter to cut rounds from them.

Although it's not traditional, we've had good luck substituting 1 tablespoon Southeast Asian fish sauce for the dried shrimp.

MUSHROOM WONTONS

This is a variation on that restaurant favorite, wontons filled with cream cheese and crab. Like many good recipes, it was an accident. Barbara discovered a lonely stir-fried portobello mushroom in the refrigerator and decided to try it as a filling for the wontons she was making. The mushroom wontons were a hit with her family. For a more conventional filling, add 1/3 cup crabmeat (or 3 shredded sticks imitation crabmeat) and 2 teaspoons curry powder to the cream cheese. These are delicious served with a ready-made sweet-and-sour sauce.

MAKES 20 WONTONS

1 tablespoon unsalted butter

1 medium to large portobello mushroom, or 3 large white or brown button mushrooms, stemmed

4 ounces cream cheese at room temperature, cut into cubes

20 wonton wrappers

3 cups peanut oil

In a wok over medium heat, melt the butter. Fry the mushroom, turning once, for 2 to 3 minutes, or until tender. Transfer the mushroom to a plate and cut it in half.

In a food processor fitted with the steel blade, process the mushroom until finely chopped. Add the cream cheese and process until mixed. Or, using a knife, finely chop the mushroom by hand and mix with the cream cheese.

To fill the wontons, have a small bowl of water near your work surface. Place a damp paper or kitchen towel over the wrappers to keep them from drying out. Place a wrapper on the work surface, one point facing downward. Place ½ to ¾ teaspoon of the filling in the center of the wrapper. Dip your fingertip in the water and run it lightly around the edge of the wrapper. Fold the top of the wrapper over the filling to make a triangle and seal the edges. Then bring the right and left corners together and seal. Repeat with the remaining wrappers and filling.

Set the wontons on a lightly floured plate and cover loosely with plastic wrap until ready to fry.

In a wok over medium-high heat, heat the oil to 375°F. Carefully slide the wontons, 6 to 8 at a time, into the hot oil, and fry for about 30 seconds per side, or until golden brown. Using a slotted spoon, remove the wontons and drain on paper towels.

Transfer the wontons to a serving plate and serve hot.

To make ahead of time: Assemble the wontons and arrange them in a single layer on a wax paper–lined baking sheet. Cover the wontons with a sheet of plastic wrap coated with nonstick cooking spray and refrigerate for up to 8 hours. Or, freeze them, uncovered, for about 1 hour, or until solid, then place them in plastic freezer bags. Seal and freeze for up to 1 month. Don't thaw them before frying. Allow an extra minute or so of frying time. The frozen wontons will sputter when they hit the hot oil, so be careful.

PORTOBELLO MUSHROOM SANDWICHES

*The rich, meaty portobello is the "bread" in this sandwich. For finger appetizers,
cut each mushroom into 4 wedges. For a luncheon, you can serve these mushroom "sandwiches" in toasted rolls.*

MAKES 8 SERVINGS
AS AN APPETIZER /
4 AS AN ENTRÉE

4 large portobello mushrooms, stemmed

4 thin slices Swiss cheese, cut a bit smaller than the mushroom caps

1 cup seasoned bread crumbs

1 tablespoon chopped fresh oregano, or 1 teaspoon dried oregano

3 tablespoons extra-virgin olive oil

1 head radicchio, leaves separated

Using a small, sharp knife, cut a horizontal slit most of the way through each mushroom cap; do not cut it all the way in half. Carefully insert a slice of cheese in the slit, cutting the cheese into 2 pieces if needed to fit it in the slit.

On a plate, combine the bread crumbs and the oregano. Brush both sides of the mushrooms with ½ tablespoon of olive oil, then roll them in the bread crumbs.

In a wok over medium-high heat, heat the remaining oil. Reduce the heat to medium. Add the mushrooms, 2 at a time, and fry, turning once, for about 4 minutes, or until lightly browned.

Arrange the radicchio leaves on a plate. Arrange the mushrooms atop the radicchio and serve.

*To make ahead of time: The mushrooms can be fried up to
30 minutes in advance and kept warm in a 200ºF oven.*

GREEN ONION BREAD

A standard on Chinese buffet tables, this bread is coiled and fried rather than baked. Rolling up and coiling the dough helps distribute the onions throughout the bread and gives it a flaky-tender texture.

MAKES 16 PIECES

2 cups all-purpose flour plus more for rolling out bread

2 tablespoons baking powder

1 cup boiling water

4 tablespoons vegetable shortening, or as needed

4 green onions, white parts and 1 to 2 inches of green parts, minced

Coarse salt for sprinkling

2 to 3 cups peanut oil

In a food processor fitted with the steel blade, combine the 2 cups of flour and the baking powder. With the machine running, pour in the boiling water in a slow, steady stream and process for a few seconds, until the dough forms a ball. To use an electric mixer: In the mixing bowl, combine the flour and baking powder on low speed and, with the machine running, pour the boiling water down the inside of the bowl. Mix until the dough forms a ball. To make the dough by hand: In a bowl, combine the flour and baking powder. Pour in the boiling water and stir until the dough is smooth. Turn it out onto a lightly floured surface and knead for about 1 minute, just to incorporate all the bits of dough.

Gather the dough into a ball, put it in a bowl, and cover the bowl with a damp cloth. Let stand in a warm, draft-free place for 30 minutes to 1 hour.

Sprinkle flour on a pastry cloth. Divide the dough into 2 equal pieces. Knead each piece for a few turns. Then, using a rolling pin covered with a pastry sleeve, continue kneading (by pounding lightly with the rolling pin) and rolling out each piece into a 10-inch circle.

Using a pastry brush, brush each dough circle with about 2 tablespoons vegetable shortening and sprinkle each with half of the green onions. Sprinkle with coarse salt. Lightly press the onions into the dough.

Roll up each circle jelly-roll style, stretching it even longer as you roll. Then form the rolled dough into a coil, starting at one end. Gently roll it out again into a 10-inch circle. Using kitchen shears, cut each circle into 8 wedges.

In a wok over medium-high heat, heat the oil to 375°F. Gently slide the wedges, 3 or 4 at a time, into the hot oil. Fry, using two forks to turn the bread once, for about 30 seconds per side, or until golden brown. Using a slotted spoon and a fork, remove the bread and drain on paper towels. Sprinkle with coarse salt and serve.

To make ahead of time: The bread can be fried up to a day ahead of time and then reheated in a 275°F oven for 5 minutes before serving.

CRAB AND ASPARAGUS SPRING ROLLS

Crab spring rolls are a staple of Vietnamese street cookery. Usually these addictive treats are made with crab and pork, but for a lighter flavor, we have substituted shrimp for the pork. To add some interest and color, we have also included asparagus in the filling. If you prefer the traditional version, replace the shrimp and asparagus with ½ pound ground lean pork.

MAKES 26 TO 30 SPRING ROLLS

3 dried shiitake mushrooms

4 ounces asparagus, trimmed

¾ pound fresh or pasteurized crabmeat, picked over

¼ pound raw shrimp, peeled, deveined, and finely chopped

2 shallots, minced

2 teaspoons minced fresh lemongrass, tender white part only

4 cloves garlic, minced

2 teaspoons grated fresh ginger

2 teaspoons fish sauce

¼ teaspoon salt

¼ teaspoon freshly ground pepper

1 egg

30 small (6-inch) rice paper wrappers (see Note)

4 cups canola or vegetable oil

Nuoc Cham (page 205) for serving

Put the mushrooms in a heatproof bowl. Add hot water to cover and soak for 30 minutes, or until soft. Drain. Trim off and discard the stems. Finely chop the caps.

Bring a saucepan of water to a boil over high heat. Add the asparagus and cook for 2 to 3 minutes, or until bright green. Drain and let cool, then cut into ⅛- to ¼-inch pieces.

In a bowl, combine the crabmeat, shrimp, chopped mushrooms, asparagus, shallots, lemongrass, garlic, ginger, fish sauce, salt, and pepper. Add the egg and mix well.

To fill the spring rolls, have a shallow plate of very warm water near your work surface. Add a rice paper round and soak for 20 to 30 seconds, or until softened, then put the wrapper on the work surface. Fold up the bottom one-fourth of the wrapper. Place 1 rounded tablespoon of the filling about ½ inch from the bottom edge. Fold the sides of the wrapper over the filling, then roll the wrapper up, making a tight bundle. Place on a sheet of plastic wrap. Repeat with the remaining wrappers and filling, replenishing the warm water as needed. (We find it handy to use two plates of water—glass pie plates are ideal. Heat one in the microwave while soaking rice paper wrappers in the other.)

Preheat an oven to 200ºF. In a wok over medium-high heat, heat the oil to 375ºF. Reduce the heat to medium. Add the spring rolls, 3 or 4 at a time, to the hot oil and fry, turning once or twice, for 5 to 7 minutes, or until golden. Using tongs, remove the spring rolls to a paper towel–lined pan and keep warm in the oven.

Serve warm with the Nuoc Cham.

To make ahead of time: Assemble the spring rolls and arrange them in a single layer on a wax paper–lined baking sheet. Cover the spring rolls with a sheet of plastic wrap coated with nonstick cooking spray and refrigerate for up to 24 hours. You can freeze them, but you have to fry them first. Place the fried spring rolls in plastic freezer bags and freeze for up to 1 month. Don't thaw them before reheating. Reheat in a 325ºF oven for 20 minutes, turning once, or until heated through.

Note: If you cannot find small rice paper wrappers, you can use the larger (8½-inch-diameter) ones. The recipe will then yield 18 to 20 spring rolls. They will need to cook for about 1 minute longer.

SPARERIBS WITH KUMQUATS

Ask the butcher to cut the ribs in half so they are about 2 inches long. These are rich and go a long way. Preserved kumquats are available in specialty-food stores and some large supermarkets, especially during the winter holidays.

MAKES 8 SERVINGS AS AN APPETIZER / 4 AS AN ENTRÉE

2 pounds pork spareribs, ribs separated and halved crosswise

½ cup cornstarch

3 cups peanut oil

1 cup preserved kumquats with some juice, or orange or kumquat marmalade thinned with a little fresh orange juice

Chopped green onions or fresh cilantro for garnishing

In a paper bag, toss the ribs with the cornstarch.

In a wok over medium-high heat, heat the oil to 375°F. Reduce the heat to medium. Carefully slide about 2 cups of the ribs into the hot oil and fry for about 5 minutes, or until the ribs are crispy and cooked through. Using a slotted spoon, remove the ribs and drain on paper towels.

Transfer the ribs to a bowl or shallow platter and sprinkle with the kumquats and some of the juice. Sprinkle with green onions and serve hot.

To make ahead of time: Fry the spareribs and refrigerate in a covered container for up to 24 hours. To reheat, place in a baking dish and cover with foil. Heat in a 350°F oven for 15 to 20 minutes, or until heated through. Sprinkle with the kumquats, kumquat juice, and green onions and serve.

CHICKEN PACKETS

Another Chinese favorite, these are deep-fried, but rather than getting crisp, the food simply cooks in the waxed paper. Diners have the fun of opening their own little packets. Although most Westerners probably don't associate cinnamon with Chinese cuisine, the Chinese long have prized the spice, and much of our cinnamon (actually cassia, from a similar shrub) comes from China.

MAKES 12 PACKETS

12 sheets of waxed paper, each cut into an 8-inch square

Dark sesame oil for brushing

12 thin slices boneless chicken breast

3 large white mushrooms, each cut into 4 slices

2 green onions, white parts only, halved lengthwise, then each half cut into 3 pieces

1½ tablespoons grated fresh ginger

Ground cinnamon for sprinkling

1 egg, lightly beaten

3 cups vegetable oil

Using a pastry brush, brush one side of each sheet of waxed paper with sesame oil. Set 1 slice of chicken in the center of the paper. Arrange 1 mushroom slice on the chicken along with 1 piece of green onion. Sprinkle with ginger and a very light dusting of cinnamon. Brush the edges of the paper with the egg. Fold up the paper envelope-style, sealing the edges. Repeat with the remaining papers and filling.

In a wok over medium-high heat, heat the oil to 375°F. Reduce the heat to medium. Carefully slide the packets, 4 at a time, into the hot oil and fry for 1 minute, then turn the packets over and fry for 2 minutes, or until the chicken turns opaque. Using a slotted spoon, remove the packets and drain on paper towels.

Serve hot, allowing diners to open their own packets.

To make ahead of time: The packets can be assembled and refrigerated for up to 8 hours. Fry them just before serving.

POLENTA FRIES WITH MANGO SALSA

Polenta, the Italian name for cooked cornmeal, is a versatile food that pairs well with many flavors. The secret to keeping it lump-free is to start with cold water. To save time, buy a ready-made log of polenta and slice it into fries.

MAKES 8 SERVINGS

3 cups cold water

1 cup finely ground white or yellow cornmeal

1 teaspoon sugar

2 tablespoons unsalted butter

1 cup all-purpose flour

1 tablespoon chopped fresh basil, or 1½ teaspoons dried

2 eggs, lightly beaten with 2 teaspoons water

3 cups vegetable oil

Mango Salsa (recipe follows) for serving

Oil an 8-by-4-inch loaf pan.

In a wok or saucepan over medium heat, pour in the cold water. Gradually add the cornmeal, whisking constantly. Continue cooking, whisking often, for 6 to 8 minutes, or until the polenta pulls away from the sides of the pan. Mix in the sugar and butter.

Spoon the polenta into the prepared pan and smooth the top with the back of a spoon. Cover with aluminum foil or plastic wrap and refrigerate for about 1 hour, or until the polenta is firm. Unmold the polenta. Cut it into ½-inch slices, and then cut the slices into ½-inch strips.

Mix the flour and basil on a plate. Put the egg mixture in a shallow bowl.

In a wok over medium-high heat, heat the oil to 375°F. Roll the polenta strips in the egg mixture and then in the flour mixture. Reduce the heat to medium. Carefully slide the polenta strips, a few at a time, into the hot oil and fry for 1 to 2 minutes, or until golden. Using a slotted spoon, remove the polenta fries and drain on paper towels.

Serve the fries hot with mango salsa.

To make ahead of time: The polenta can be cooked in advance and refrigerated for up to 2 days. Fry the polenta strips just before serving.

MANGO SALSA

This recipe can be doubled or tripled. To save time, you can buy peeled and sliced mangoes in a jar in the produce section. You'll need about 2 cups chopped mango. This salsa is best served the same day you make it.

MAKES 8 SERVINGS

2 mangoes, pitted and peeled

1 medium orange bell pepper, seeded, deribbed, and chopped

1 medium onion, chopped

⅓ cup chopped fresh cilantro

1 small serrano chile, seeded and chopped

⅓ cup fresh lime juice

Chop the mango pulp and put it in a nonreactive bowl. Add the bell pepper, onion, cilantro, chile, and lime juice, and toss gently.

Cover the salsa loosely with plastic wrap and refrigerate until ready to serve. Toss again before serving.

FLOWERPOT ONION RINGS

Crispy and both sweet and pungent, "onion blossoms"—onion rings served in a pile that the guests pick apart as they munch—are a favorite at many family-style restaurants. The fried onion rings can be served separately and not molded into the pot shape, but this is such an easy way to make a decorative presentation. Just be sure to use a clean, new pot— not the one that held your geraniums last summer.

MAKES 8 SERVINGS

1 new 4-inch clay flowerpot

3 large onions

1 cup all-purpose flour

½ cup cornmeal

½ teaspoon salt, plus more as needed

¼ teaspoon freshly ground white pepper

4 cups peanut oil

Wash the flowerpot in soapy water, rinse well, and drain.

Cut the onions into ¼-inch slices and separate them into rings.

In a brown paper bag, combine the flour, cornmeal, the ½ teaspoon salt, and the white pepper and shake to mix. Working in batches, add the onion rings and shake to coat with the flour mixture.

In a wok over medium-high heat, heat the oil to 375ºF. Working in batches, fry the onion rings for 1 to 2 minutes, or until golden brown. Using a slotted spoon, remove the onions and drain on paper towels. Continue until all of the onions have been cooked and drained.

Put the onions in the flowerpot, packing them lightly. Invert the pot onto a serving dish to release the onions. Serve immediately. Let the diners use forks to separate the onions, and pass the salt.

To make ahead of time: The onion rings don't have to be served piping hot, so you can fry them and keep them warm in a 250ºF oven for a few minutes while you prepare the other party foods for serving. Pack the onion rings in the flowerpot just before serving.

CHINESE-STYLE STUFFED PEPPERS

You'll find these delightful tidbits on dim sum carts everywhere. We sometimes call them "down-side-up stuffed peppers" because you cook them filling-side down, then serve them filling-side up.

MAKES 12 PIECES

Sauce

½ cup cold water

1 tablespoon soy sauce

1 teaspoon cornstarch

1 teaspoon sugar

2 medium red or green bell peppers

Filling

6 ounces ground lean pork

1 teaspoon grated fresh ginger

¼ cup minced water chestnuts

1 green onion, white part only, minced

2 tablespoons dry white wine

1½ tablespoons soy sauce

¼ teaspoon salt

1 cup cornstarch

3 tablespoons peanut oil

To make the sauce: In a small bowl, whisk together the water, soy sauce, cornstarch, and sugar. Set aside.

Cut the bell peppers in half lengthwise, discarding the ribs and seeds. Then cut each half lengthwise into thirds to make 12 pieces. Set aside.

To make the filling: In a bowl, combine the pork, ginger, water chestnuts, green onion, wine, soy sauce, and salt.

Press the pork mixture evenly over the cut sides of the peppers. Spread the cornstarch on a plate and dredge the peppers, filling-side down, in the cornstarch. Put the peppers on a plate and set aside.

In a wok over medium-high heat, heat the oil and swirl it around to coat the wok. Add the stuffed peppers, filling-side down, and fry for 3 minutes, or until the filling is crusted and golden brown. Move the peppers around with a spatula so they will all have been in the center of the wok.

Add the sauce, cover the wok, and simmer for 10 minutes. Using a spatula, remove the peppers and set them, filling-side up, on a serving dish. Drizzle with the sauce. Serve hot.

To make ahead of time: The peppers can be fried 30 to 40 minutes in advance and kept warm in a 200°F oven. Add the sauce just before serving.

MUSHROOM AND LEEK BUNDLES

This is "mu shu" with a Western-style filling. Vary the mushrooms according to the season and your taste. Try shiitakes or even morels or fresh porcini. If desired, you can accompany the bundles with sour cream or yogurt, seasoned with a bit of fresh dill. These are substantial and need be served only with another tidbit or two to make a dim sum meal.

MAKES 4 SERVINGS

2 to 3 tablespoons olive oil

1 tablespoon unsalted butter

3 leeks, white parts only, sliced lengthwise, thoroughly cleaned,
    and cut crosswise into thin slices

1 pound brown mushrooms, thinly sliced

8 ounces white button mushrooms or another variety of your choice, thinly sliced

1 cup grated carrots

2 tablespoons cornstarch

3 tablespoons vegetable broth or cold water

1 cup cooked and cooled wild, brown, or white rice

1 teaspoon dried thyme

Salt and freshly ground pepper

4 warmed flour tortillas, preferably tomato- or spinach-flavored, or Asian
    Pancakes (page 202)

To add an elegant touch, reserve the green leek tops and cut them into very narrow strips. Blanch or stir-fry them briefly to soften them, then use the leek strips as "ribbons" to tie around the bundles. Tuck a raw enoki mushroom into each leek "ribbon."

In a wok over medium-high heat, heat the oil and melt the butter. Add the leeks and stir-fry for 2 to 3 minutes, or until tender and just beginning to brown. Add the mushrooms and carrots and cook for 3 to 4 minutes, or until the mushrooms are cooked through but not mushy.

In a bowl, whisk together the cornstarch and the vegetable broth and stir the mixture into the mushrooms. Continue cooking, stirring, for about 1 minute, or until the liquid thickens. Stir in the rice, thyme, and salt and pepper to taste.

Set a tortilla on a plate and spoon some of the mushroom-leek mixture down the center. Fold one side over the filling, then fold in the top and bottom and roll the filled tortilla to make a neat bundle. Repeat with the remaining tortillas and filling. Serve immediately.

To make ahead of time: You can prepare the filling up to a day in advance; cover and refrigerate it. Just before serving, reheat the filling and fill and fold the tortillas.

STEAMED EGGPLANT

Added as an aromatic to the steaming water, ginger imparts a subtle flavor to the eggplant.
Delicious hot or cold, this is a natural for a buffet.

MAKES 8 SERVINGS

4 slices fresh ginger

2 medium eggplants (about 2 pounds total), peeled and each cut into 8 wedges

Sauce

6 tablespoons cider vinegar

6 tablespoons firmly packed light brown sugar

2 teaspoons dark sesame oil

2 tablespoons soy sauce

4 cloves garlic, minced

2 tablespoons grated fresh ginger

Regular or black sesame seeds for garnishing (optional)

Fill a wok one-half to two-thirds full of water and bring to a boil over high heat. Add the ginger slices, reduce the heat to medium, and fit an oiled steamer rack or bamboo steamer in the wok. If using a bamboo steamer, set an oiled heatproof plate in it. Arrange the eggplant wedges on the rack or plate. Cover and steam for 10 to 15 minutes, or until the eggplant is cooked through and soft.

Meanwhile, make the sauce: In a small bowl, whisk together the vinegar, sugar, sesame oil, soy sauce, garlic, and ginger.

Using tongs, transfer the eggplant wedges to a plate. Drizzle the sauce over the eggplant and sprinkle with sesame seeds, if using. Serve hot or cold.

To make ahead of time: The eggplant can be steamed, sauced, and refrigerated, covered, for up to 2 days. Sprinkle with sesame seeds just before serving.

CHAPTER THREE

STIR CRAZY

THE ART OF STIR-FRYING

JUST SAY "WOK" AND MOST PEOPLE THINK OF STIR-FRYING. AND INDEED, THIS PAN WAS BORN TO STIR-FRY. BOTH THE WOK AND STIR-FRYING ORIGINATED IN CHINA. WHILE NOBODY CAN PINPOINT THE PRECISE ORIGINS OF STIR-FRYING, THIS TECHNIQUE OF CUTTING FOOD INTO BITS AND COOKING IT QUICKLY OVER HIGH HEAT IS AT LEAST TWO THOUSAND YEARS OLD AND PROBABLY CAUGHT FIRE AS THE ANSWER TO FUEL SHORTAGES. WOOD FOR COOKING COULD BE SCARCE IN SOME AREAS OF CHINA, AND STIR-FRYING REQUIRES SO LITTLE OF IT. NOTHING BEATS THE WOK AS A STIR-FRYING VESSEL. THE BOTTOM OF THE PAN GETS REALLY HOT, AND THE DEEP SIDES ALLOW YOU TO TOSS THE INGREDIENTS VIGOROUSLY WITHOUT WORRYING THAT BITS OF YOUR MEAL WILL FLY AROUND THE STOVE.

The Chinese exported the wok and the art of stir-frying to countries such as Vietnam, Thailand, and Indonesia, and more recently to the United States, Canada, and other Western lands. Stir-frying appeals to cooks and diners for several reasons. It's the original fast-food technique; a hot wok helps you get dinner on the table in minutes. It's healthful; the quick cooking ensures that foods retain vitamins. And it's downright appealing to the palate; meats stay tender and vegetables, crisp and colorful.

There are three essential elements to a great stir-fry: preparation, heat, and attention.

Preparation
The first bit of magic behind successful stir-frying is to have all the ingredients prepared and at hand, including the sauce. You don't want to be frantically chopping peppers or digging around for the cornstarch while the meat turns into scorched shoe leather. We often find it handy to chop or slice the vegetables early in the day or even a day in advance. Better yet, we "cheat" with high-quality washed, trimmed, and bagged fresh produce such as broccoli florets, baby carrots, sugar snap peas, and shredded cabbage.

Cut the food into small, fairly uniform pieces. Even if you don't eat with chopsticks, small pieces of food cook more quickly and evenly than larger ones, and cutting the ingredients uniformly gives the dish a pleasing symmetry. So for a noodle dish, you might cut the meat and vegetables into long strips, while for a dish that includes peanuts, you would dice the other ingredients. Of course, sometimes you might deliberately flout this guideline to add contrast to the dish.

To make slicing meats and poultry easier, first freeze them for a half-hour to an hour, or until they are firm but not frozen solid. Then slice them against the grain.

As a sauce sits, the ingredients (especially cornstarch) may separate. Just before adding it to the wok, whisk or stir the sauce again.

Heat

The Chinese distill the art of stir-frying into a phrase: "Hot wok, cold oil." To keep foods from sticking and to cook them rapidly, put the wok on the burner and crank up the heat to high. Note that this is not a good idea with most nonstick-coated woks, which is why we recommend using them primarily for stir-frying starchy, sticky foods such as noodles and rice, where the advantages of the nonstick coating offset its aversion to high heat.

When the wok is so hot that it's beginning to smoke, pour in the oil and swirl the pan (carefully!) to coat the bottom and sides. Then start adding the food. This is the method for uncoated metal woks. For a wok with a nonstick coating, do the reverse—add the oil, then heat the pan over medium-high to high heat. (Read the manufacturer's directions to determine the best heat level.)

Pay Attention

Finally, once you have the food in the pan, pay attention. Stir-frying is fast. A difference of a minute or two separates a perfectly cooked stir-fry from an overcooked mass of tough meat and limp vegetables. When you're stir-frying garlic, literally a second separates fragrant from acrid. As Barbara's first Chinese cooking instructor, Mai Leung, long ago cautioned her, once that stir-fry is in the pan, do not answer the phone. That's still good advice, even in the age of hands-free cell and cordless phones. And wait until your partner or spouse walks through the door before you heat up the wok to cook dinner.

More Stir-Frying Tips

Other important details affect the final stir-fried dish. One is oil. For stir-frying and deep-frying, Chinese restaurants and classical cooks long have favored peanut oil, with its full flavor and high smoking point. It is, indeed, just about the best all-around oil for frying, although most refined vegetable oils with a smoking point of at least 400°F (see page 105) are fine for stir-frying. We've used olive (regular), corn, canola, soybean, and walnut oils with good results. We use butter sparingly in a few stir-fried dishes. Browned butter tastes great—just be sure to add the food quickly to keep the butter from scorching. In a few recipes, we use extra-virgin olive oil for its incomparable flavor. Because the oil breaks down quickly over high heat, do not let the pan get too hot.

Don't crowd the wok, especially when stir-frying meats. If you put too much food in the pan, the ingredients will simmer rather than fry. Stir-fry meats in small batches, removing one batch to a plate before you stir-fry the rest. Once all the meat is cooked and the sauce is bubbling away, you can return all the meat to the wok to coat it with the sauce.

Another consideration is the order in which foods are stir-fried. For both aesthetic and practical reasons, traditional stir-frying often calls for vegetables and meats to be cooked separately before being combined and sauced. In many recipes, we have overruled tradition in favor of convenience. To save a little cooking and cleanup time, we often stir-fry meats and vegetables together.

How starches work with frying is also important. In a number of recipes, we follow the classic Asian technique of dusting the meat or poultry with cornstarch before adding it to the wok. When the food hits the hot oil, this coating creates a "mini-batter" that helps seal in juices and keep the meat tender.

The recipes in this chapter often call for cooking ginger, garlic, or green onions "until fragrant." We mean that literally. When the ginger or garlic begins to sizzle and give off an aroma—seconds after it hits the oil—it's time to add the next ingredient.

Barbara still remembers the first time she stir-fried a meal for guests. Accustomed to European and American cooking methods, she experienced a moment of panic as she realized the guests would be arriving in a few minutes and her house smelled like ... nothing. No baking bread, no simmering sauces. She felt as though she had forgotten something. Of course, once all the ingredients hit the wok, the glorious smells wafted everywhere. She has been happily stir-frying ever since.

BEEF WITH ASPARAGUS AND WALNUTS

Fresh white asparagus has begun popping up in some supermarkets and specialty markets, especially in larger cities. Occasionally, you may even spy purple asparagus. For a touch of class, make this stir-fry with a combination of green and white asparagus, green and purple asparagus, or even all three. This is good with cooked noodles or rice.

MAKES 4 SERVINGS

Sauce

⅓ cup oyster sauce

1 teaspoon sugar

2 tablespoons dry white wine

1 to 1¼ pounds beef flank steak, cut into thin strips

2 tablespoons soy sauce

3 tablespoons cornstarch

2 to 3 tablespoons peanut oil

3 cloves garlic, minced

2 teaspoons grated fresh ginger

6 green onions, white part only, chopped

1 pound asparagus, trimmed and cut into 1-inch pieces

½ cup chopped walnuts, preferably toasted (see page 209)

To make the sauce: In a small bowl, combine the oyster sauce, sugar, and wine. Set aside.

In a bowl, sprinkle the beef with the soy sauce and cornstarch. Toss lightly and set aside.

Heat a wok over medium-high to high heat. Pour in the oil. Add the garlic, ginger, and green onions and stir-fry for a few seconds, or until fragrant. Add the beef and asparagus and stir-fry for 2 to 4 minutes, or until the beef is just cooked through. Stir in the sauce and mix well. Cook for 1 minute, or until heated through.

Mound the beef and asparagus in a serving bowl, sprinkle with the walnuts, and serve immediately.

VIETNAMESE-STYLE BEEF WITH LEMONGRASS

In Vietnam, many dishes arrive at the table accompanied by a plate heaped high with raw, fresh greens, including herbs. You can substitute basil for the mint if you like. Lemongrass is available both fresh and dried, but fresh is needed for this recipe. Accompany the beef with cooked rice noodles and a leaf-lettuce salad.

MAKES 4 SERVINGS

Sauce

3 tablespoons minced fresh lemongrass, tender white part only

3 tablespoons fresh lime juice

⅓ cup fish sauce or soy sauce

3 cloves garlic, minced

1 small red chile, minced, or ¼ teaspoon red pepper flakes, or to taste

1¼ to 1½ pounds beef top sirloin or flank steak, cut into thin strips

1½ tablespoons firmly packed light brown sugar

2 tablespoons peanut oil

¼ cup chopped shallots

1 teaspoon sesame seeds

½ cup chopped fresh mint

To make the sauce: In a small bowl, combine the lemongrass, lime juice, fish sauce, garlic, and chile. Set aside.

In a bowl, sprinkle the beef with the brown sugar. Set aside.

Heat a wok over medium-high to high heat. Pour in the oil. Add the shallots and stir-fry for a few seconds, or until fragrant. Add the beef and stir-fry for about 3 minutes, or until just cooked through. Stir in the sauce and cook for 1 minute, or until heated through.

Transfer the beef to a serving bowl, sprinkle with the sesame seeds, and garnish with the mint. Serve immediately.

SATURDAY-NIGHT SAUSAGES, POTATOES, AND RED PEPPERS

This dish makes a great weekend supper. If you enjoy more spice in your life, use hot Italian sausages.
It's good as is or served over hot pasta.

MAKES 4 TO 6 SERVINGS

4 medium boiling potatoes (about 1 pound total)

2 tablespoons olive oil

1 large onion, sliced

4 or 5 mild Italian sausages, cut into ½-inch slices

3 red bell peppers, seeded, deribbed, and sliced

2 teaspoons chopped fresh oregano, or 1 teaspoon dried oregano

Fill a wok half full of salted water and bring to a boil over high heat.

Add the potatoes and cook for about 15 minutes, or until almost tender. Drain and let stand until cool enough to handle, then cut the potatoes into slices.

In a wok, preferably nonstick, over medium-high heat, heat the oil. Add the onion and sausages and cook for 4 to 5 minutes, or until evenly browned. Add the potatoes and the bell peppers (and the oregano, if you are using dried). Cook, stirring occasionally, for about 2 minutes, or until the potatoes are golden brown and the sausages are cooked through. Sprinkle with the fresh oregano (unless you are using dried). Serve immediately.

PORK, FENNEL, AND BLOOD ORANGES

Their gorgeous rosy-hued flesh and slightly perfumed citrus flavor make blood oranges a real treat, even if they're now a supermarket staple instead of an exotic import. They're a perfect foil for the rich flavor of pork and the anise tones of fennel. If blood oranges are not available, use tangelos or regular oranges.

MAKES 4 SERVINGS

4 medium to large blood oranges, or small-medium tangelos

1½ tablespoons cornstarch

½ cup chicken broth, or as needed

1 large fennel bulb

1 pound pork tenderloin, cut into very thin slices

¼ teaspoon salt

¼ teaspoon freshly ground black pepper

3 tablespoons peanut oil or olive oil

¼ to ½ teaspoon red pepper flakes

4 cloves garlic, minced

1 tablespoon rice vinegar or balsamic vinegar

2 teaspoons sugar

Grate the zest and squeeze the juice from 2 of the oranges; you should have ⅓ to ½ cup juice. Peel the remaining 2 oranges, carefully scraping off as much of the white pith as possible, then cut into thick slices. Remove any seeds. Set the zest and orange slices aside.

In a bowl, whisk together 1 tablespoon of the cornstarch and the orange juice, then add enough chicken broth to make 1 cup. Set aside.

Trim the stalks and leaves from the fennel (save them to flavor soups). Halve the bulb lengthwise, then core and cut lengthwise into thin slices. Set aside.

In a bowl, sprinkle the pork with the remaining ½ tablespoon cornstarch, the salt, and black pepper. Toss lightly and set aside.

Heat a wok over medium-high to high heat. Pour in 1 tablespoon of the oil. Add the fennel and stir-fry for 2 to 3 minutes, or until glossy and just beginning to soften, adding a little water if the fennel begins to look dry. Using a slotted spoon, transfer the fennel to a plate.

Add the remaining 2 tablespoons oil to the wok, then add the pork, the orange zest, red pepper flakes to taste, and the garlic. Stir-fry for 2 to 4 minutes, or until the pork is just cooked through. Stir in the orange juice mixture, vinegar, and sugar. Cook for 1 to 2 minutes, or until the sauce thickens and turns clear.

Spoon the pork onto a platter and surround with the fennel and the orange slices. Serve immediately.

STIR-FRIED CHICKEN WITH LITCHI AND PAPAYA

It's the dead of March. Nothing seems to be in season anywhere in the world. The citrus is still good, but if you see one more orange . . . This is when you realize why canned, bottled, and frozen fruits and vegetables were invented. We favor those colorful bottled fruits in the produce section, especially papaya and mango. Fresh litchis are still fairly rare in America's heartland, so we almost always use canned ones. If you do find fresh litchis, by all means use them. Serve this stir-fry over cooked rice.

MAKES 4 SERVINGS

1 can (11 ounces) litchis, drained, ¼ cup juice reserved

2 tablespoons cornstarch

2 tablespoons peanut oil

3 green onions, white parts only, chopped

2 teaspoons grated fresh ginger

1 pound boneless, skinless chicken breasts, cut into thin strips

3 tablespoons soy sauce

2 tablespoons dry white wine

4 ounces snow peas or sugar snap peas

1 cup sliced fresh or bottled, drained papaya

In a small bowl, whisk together the litchi juice and cornstarch. Set aside.

Heat a wok over medium-high to high heat. Pour in the oil. Add the green onions and ginger and stir-fry for about 1 minute, or until the onions soften and are fragrant. Add the chicken and stir-fry for about 3 minutes, or until it is just cooked through. Add the soy sauce and wine. Mix in the snow peas, litchis, and papaya. Add the litchi juice mixture and continue cooking, stirring, for 1 to 2 minutes, or until the snow peas are bright green and the sauce thickens and turns clear. Serve immediately.

THAI-STYLE BASIL CHICKEN

Thai (or holy) basil, with its sharp licorice flavor, is best for this stir-fry, a popular dish found on nearly every Thai restaurant menu. But regular sweet basil will work. If your supermarket doesn't carry fish sauce, the salty, pungent condiment indispensable for much of Southeast Asian cooking, you'll have to visit or order from an Asian market. It's worth the time and trouble. Serve this dish with lime wedges and hot rice.

MAKES 4 SERVINGS

2 tablespoons peanut oil

¼ cup minced shallots

3 cloves garlic, minced

¼ teaspoon red pepper flakes, or to taste

1 pound boneless, skinless chicken breasts, cut into ½-inch-wide strips

1 jar (7 ounces) baby corn, drained and rinsed

¼ cup fish sauce

¼ cup fresh lime juice

1 cup fresh basil leaves, preferably Thai basil

Salt and freshly ground black pepper

Heat a wok over medium-high to high heat. Pour in the oil. Add the shallots, garlic, and red pepper flakes and stir-fry for about 1 minute, or until the shallots are tender. Add the chicken and stir-fry for 2 to 3 minutes, or until just cooked through. Add the corn. Mix in the fish sauce, lime juice, and basil. Season with salt and black pepper to taste. Serve immediately.

CHICKEN WITH BLACK BEAN AND GARLIC SAUCE

One of the big stars in the Chinese culinary firmament, black beans are fermented, dried, and salted soybeans. Their winy-salty flavor resembles that of soy sauce but is deeper. Black beans often are used as a foil to delicately flavored ingredients such as chicken and seafood. You're most likely to find black beans in a bottled sauce, usually with garlic. Serve this dish with cooked rice.

MAKES 4 SERVINGS

2 tablespoons peanut oil

1 tablespoon peeled, minced fresh ginger

3 tablespoons black bean and garlic sauce

4 green onions, white part only, chopped

2 tablespoons soy sauce

¼ cup chicken broth mixed with 1 teaspoon cornstarch

2 whole boneless, skinless chicken breasts (about 1 pound total), cut into ½-inch-wide strips

2 red or green bell peppers, seeded, deribbed, and cut into strips

Heat a wok over medium-high to high heat. Pour in the oil. Add the ginger, black bean sauce, and green onions, and stir-fry for about 1 minute, or until bubbly and fragrant. Stir in the soy sauce and chicken broth mixture. Add the chicken and bell peppers and stir-fry for 2 to 3 minutes, or until the chicken is just cooked through and the peppers are tender-crisp. Serve immediately.

Variation: Substitute 3 or 4 bunches of baby bok choy for the bell peppers. Keep the small leaves whole and cut the large ones lengthwise into 2 or 3 pieces.

CHICKEN WITH HEARTS OF ROMAINE

We have never understood why Chinese restaurants in the United States so seldom serve stir-fried lettuce, especially given how commonplace it is on restaurant menus in southern China. Lettuce takes on a whole new personality when delicately seasoned and lightly cooked. We've added chicken to make it a main dish. This was a hit with Virginia's children, who turn up their noses at other cooked greens such as spinach and kale. It's good with rice or noodles.

MAKES 4 SERVINGS

Sauce

1 tablespoon oyster sauce

1 tablespoon dry white wine

¾ cup chicken broth

1 tablespoon cornstarch

12 ounces hearts of Romaine (about 2 medium heads)

2 tablespoons vegetable oil

2 teaspoons grated fresh ginger

2 cloves garlic, minced

1 pound boneless, skinless chicken breasts, cut into ½-inch-wide strips

To make the sauce: In a bowl, whisk together the oyster sauce, wine, chicken broth, and cornstarch. Set aside.

Separate the lettuce leaves. Keep the small leaves whole. Cut the large leaves in half crosswise, then in half again lengthwise. Set aside.

Heat a wok over medium-high to high heat. Pour in the oil. Add the ginger and garlic and stir-fry for a few seconds, or until fragrant. Add the chicken and stir-fry for 2 to 3 minutes, or until just cooked through. Stir in the sauce and cook for 1 to 2 minutes, or until the sauce thickens and turns clear. Add the lettuce and stir-fry just until the lettuce wilts. Serve immediately.

SHRIMP IN LOBSTER SAUCE

This Chinese-restaurant favorite includes no lobster. It's so-named because the sauce is similar to one the Chinese serve with lobster. Accompany with cooked white rice.

MAKES 4 SERVINGS

1 to 1¼ pounds raw jumbo shrimp, peeled and deveined

2 tablespoons dry white wine

4 tablespoons cornstarch

¾ cup cold water

2 to 4 tablespoons peanut oil

2 cloves garlic, minced

1 teaspoon grated fresh ginger

2½ tablespoons black bean and garlic sauce

¼ pound ground lean pork

2 tablespoons soy sauce

1 egg, lightly beaten

Pat the shrimp dry with paper towels and put them in a bowl. Toss the shrimp with the wine and 2 tablespoons of the cornstarch. Set aside.

In a bowl, whisk together the remaining 2 tablespoons cornstarch and ¼ cup of the water. Set aside.

Heat a wok over medium-high to high heat. Pour in 2 tablespoons oil. Add the shrimp and stir-fry for about 2 minutes, or until just opaque; do not overcook. Transfer the shrimp to a plate.

If the wok is dry, add another 2 tablespoons oil. Add the garlic, ginger, and black bean sauce. Stir-fry for a few seconds, or until fragrant. Add the pork and stir-fry for 2 to 3 minutes, or until no longer pink. Stir in the soy sauce and the remaining ½ cup water. Bring the mixture to a boil. Stir in the cornstarch mixture. Reduce the heat to low and simmer for 2 minutes. Stir in the shrimp and egg. Cover and cook for about 2 minutes, then stir. Serve immediately.

SHRIMP AND SWEET POTATO HASH

The rich sweetness of sweet potatoes is a perfect foil for the brininess of shrimp. Rock shrimp, which is a hard-shelled, deep-water cousin of the more familiar pink, brown, and white shrimp, is often available at seafood markets or supermarkets. If you can't find rock shrimp, you can substitute regular, medium, shelled shrimp.

MAKES 4 SERVINGS

3 tablespoons peanut oil

1 small red onion, minced

½ pound raw shelled rock shrimp

1 cup cooked and mashed sweet potatoes (fresh or canned and drained)

½ teaspoon grated fresh ginger

Salt and freshly ground pepper

3 to 4 handfuls assorted mixed baby greens (about 3 ounces)

⅓ cup chopped fresh chives or a handful of whole fresh chives

In a nonstick wok over medium-high heat, heat the oil. Add the onion and stir-fry for a few seconds, or until fragrant. Add the shrimp and stir-fry for 2 to 3 minutes, or until opaque. Mix in the mashed sweet potatoes, ginger, and salt and pepper to taste. Cook 1 to 2 minutes, or until heated through.

Divide the greens among 4 plates. Mound the shrimp hash atop the greens and garnish with the chopped chives. If you are using whole chives, arrange them decoratively on top of or alongside the hash. Serve immediately.

MOJO-MARINATED SCALLOPS

The Cuban vinaigrette called mojo *(pronounced MO-ho), often used to marinate pork before roasting, is delicious with all sorts of foods, including seafood. The seasonings vary—cumin and black pepper are popular—but the standard recipe contains sour orange juice (which you can approximate with a combination of orange and lime juice), olive oil, and lots of garlic. If you can get fresh sour oranges, squeeze 3 or 4 of them and skip the lime juice. Serve the scallops over cooked noodles or brown rice, or on a bed of fresh baby spinach.*

MAKES 4 SERVINGS

1 to 1¼ pounds large sea scallops

Mojo (recipe follows)

2 tablespoons olive oil

3 cloves garlic, minced

1 large cooked potato, cut into ¼-inch slices

1 large orange, peeled and quartered

2 cups baby spinach, washed

2 tablespoons fresh lime juice

Salt and freshly ground pepper

In a nonreactive bowl, combine the scallops with enough mojo to cover them. Cover and refrigerate for 2 hours. Drain.

Heat a wok over medium-high to high heat. Pour in the oil. Add the scallops and stir-fry for 2 to 3 minutes, or until opaque. Transfer the scallops to a plate.

Reheat the wok over medium-high heat. Add the garlic and stir-fry for a few seconds, or until fragrant. Add the potato slices and stir-fry for about 3 minutes, or until golden brown. Add the orange and spinach and stir-fry for about 1 minute, or until the spinach has just wilted. Return the scallops to the wok and cook for 1 minute, or until heated through. Sprinkle with the lime juice and salt and pepper to taste. Serve immediately.

MOJO

MAKES ABOUT 2 CUPS

¼ cup extra-virgin olive oil

10 cloves garlic, minced

Juice of 2 oranges

Juice of 3 limes

½ teaspoon ground cumin

¼ cup minced fresh cilantro

½ teaspoon cayenne pepper, ½ small serrano chile, minced, or ¼ teaspoon minced habañero chile (optional)

Salt

In a saucepan or small wok over medium heat, warm the olive oil. Add the garlic and cook, stirring frequently, for 4 to 5 minutes, or until the oil is infused with the garlic flavor and aroma.

Pour the garlic-infused oil into a medium nonreactive bowl. Stir or whisk in the orange juice and lime juice. Stir in the cumin, cilantro, cayenne pepper (if using), and salt to taste. Pour the mojo into a clean glass jar. Cover and refrigerate for up to 3 weeks, shaking occasionally.

SALT AND PEPPER SOFT-SHELLED CRABS

A stunning example of "less is more," this dish is simple but heavenly. Popular throughout Vietnam (and in Vietnamese restaurants abroad), salt and pepper crab must be made with the freshest of seafood. We use soft-shelled crabs because they're readily available throughout the United States during their season (late spring through early summer) and require little preparation. If soft-shelled crabs are not in season, you can use jumbo shrimp.

MAKES 4 SERVINGS

8 medium to large soft-shelled crabs, cleaned, or 1½ pounds raw jumbo shrimp, peeled and deveined (see Note)

Cornstarch for dusting

3 tablespoons peanut oil

1 tablespoon unsalted butter

1 tablespoon minced garlic

Salt, preferably coarse kosher or sea salt

Freshly coarse-ground or cracked pepper

Nuoc Cham (page 205) for serving

Pat the crabs dry and dust lightly with cornstarch.

Heat a wok over medium-high to high heat. Pour in the oil and add the butter. Add the garlic and stir-fry for a few seconds, or until fragrant. Add the crabs and stir-fry for 3 to 4 minutes, or until bright red and cooked through. Sprinkle generously with salt and pepper, toss, and serve immediately with the Nuoc Cham for dipping.

Note: If you live on the coast or have a top-notch fish market nearby, you can use 8 fresh hard-shelled blue crabs or 2 to 4 Dungeness crabs. Drop them into boiling water first (just long enough to kill them), remove the claws, and use a cleaver to crack the bodies into 2 to 4 pieces, depending on the size of the crabs. Stir-fry them immediately. You can use the same technique with lobster.

SALMON AND ARTICHOKE HEARTS WITH WALNUT PESTO AND ORZO

*This is a great way to use up leftover salmon. Cooked shrimp or diced chicken is also delicious.
If you can find fresh baby artichokes, trim them, halve them lengthwise, and use them in place of the frozen artichoke hearts.
Because they'll need to cook a bit longer, add them a minute or two before you add the salmon.*

MAKES 4 TO 6 SERVINGS

Pesto

1 cup fresh basil leaves

3 cloves garlic, halved

½ cup walnut pieces

½ cup extra-virgin olive oil

⅓ cup freshly grated Parmesan cheese

Salt and freshly ground pepper

8 ounces orzo

2 tablespoons vegetable oil

2 large shallots, chopped

9 ounces frozen artichoke hearts, thawed and halved

1½ cups cooked, boned, and flaked salmon

¼ cup capers, including juice

To make the pesto: In a food processor fitted with the steel blade, process the basil, garlic, and walnuts until ground. With the machine running, pour in the oil in a slow, steady stream until all the ingredients are combined. Add the cheese and salt and pepper to taste. Process for a couple of seconds, just to combine the ingredients.

Spoon the pesto into a small bowl, cover, and refrigerate until ready to use. Stir before using.

Fill a wok half full of salted water and bring to a boil over high heat. Add the orzo and cook for 6 to 10 minutes, or according to the package directions. Drain and set aside.

Heat a wok over medium-high to high heat. Pour in the oil. Add the shallots and stir-fry for 1 to 2 minutes, or until fragrant and tender. Add the artichoke hearts and salmon. Stir-fry for 1 to 2 minutes, or until hot. Stir in the capers. Add the orzo and pesto to taste (you may have some left over) and toss.

Spoon the orzo mixture into a serving bowl. Serve immediately, or refrigerate and bring to room temperature before serving.

PARSLIED TUNA AND NEW POTATOES

Fresh tuna has a meaty texture and a less "fishy" flavor than canned. It stands up well to the sunny, assertive Mediterranean flavors of lemon, parsley, and olives. This dish can be served hot or cold.

MAKES 4 SERVINGS

1½ pounds new potatoes (the smaller, the better), halved

2 tuna steaks (5 to 6 ounces each), cut into ½-inch-wide strips

Juice of 1 lemon

3 or 4 cloves garlic, minced

1 tablespoon extra-virgin olive oil, plus more for drizzling

1 tablespoon olive or canola oil

⅓ cup chopped fresh flat-leaf parsley

Salt and freshly ground pepper

Lemon wedges for garnishing (optional)

Black olives for garnishing (optional)

Fill a large wok two-thirds full of salted water and bring to a boil over high heat. Add the potatoes and simmer for 8 to 10 minutes, or until fork-tender but still firm. Drain and set aside.

Meanwhile, in a nonreactive dish, toss the tuna with the lemon juice, garlic, and the 1 tablespoon extra-virgin olive oil. Set aside.

In a wok, preferably nonstick, over medium-high heat, heat the olive oil. Add the potatoes and stir-fry for 2 to 3 minutes. Add the tuna along with its marinade and stir-fry for 3 to 5 minutes, or until the potatoes are browned and the tuna is just cooked through.

Add the parsley, toss to mix, and drizzle with a little extra-virgin olive oil. Season with salt and pepper to taste. Garnish with lemon wedges and olives, if using. Serve immediately, or refrigerate for up to 12 hours and serve slightly cold.

EGG FOO YONG SCRAMBLE

As a child, Barbara's daughter would not eat eggs unless they were "Chinese eggs," cooked in a wok.
Wok-cooked eggs remained one of the special treats of her childhood. This versatile dish is excellent for breakfast,
as a first course, or as a light lunch or supper entrée.

MAKES 4 TO 6 SERVINGS

Sauce

¾ cup beef broth

2 tablespoons cornstarch mixed with 2 tablespoons cold water

2 tablespoons soy sauce

½ cup frozen green peas

Eggs

6 eggs

1 teaspoon grated fresh ginger

½ teaspoon salt

1 cup cooked small shrimp

1 cup fresh bean sprouts

½ cup minced green onions, white part only

2 tablespoons peanut oil

To make the sauce: In a small wok or saucepan over medium heat, heat the beef broth. Stir in the cornstarch mixture, soy sauce, and peas. Cook, stirring, for 1 to 2 minutes, or until the sauce thickens and turns clear. Reheat just before serving.

To prepare the eggs: In a large bowl, lightly beat the eggs. Mix in the ginger, salt, shrimp, bean sprouts, and green onions.

In a nonstick wok over medium-high heat, heat the oil. Spoon the egg mixture into the wok. Turn the mixture with a spatula and cook, scrambling the eggs, for 1 to 2 minutes, or until golden.

Drizzle the eggs with the sauce and serve immediately.

PINTO BEAN CONFETTI

This flavorful, colorful dish, flecked with bits of peppers and green onions, makes an ideal vegetarian main course.
If you find chili beans seasoned with chipotle (dried, smoked jalapeño) in your supermarket,
use them in this dish. They're delicious.

MAKES 4 SERVINGS

2 cans (15 to 15½ ounces each) pinto beans, or chili beans with chipotle

2 tablespoons extra-virgin olive oil

3 cloves garlic, minced

3 green onions, white part only, finely sliced

2 red or yellow bell peppers, or a combination, seeded, deribbed, and finely diced

1 small fresh serrano or jalapeño chile, finely chopped

2 teaspoons ground cumin (if using regular pinto beans)

2 teaspoons chili powder (if using regular pinto beans)

Salt and freshly ground pepper

Sour cream

1 Haas avocado, pitted, peeled, and chopped

Tortilla chips for serving

1 lime, cut into wedges

If using regular pinto beans, drain and rinse them, then drain again. If using chili beans, drain but don't rinse them.

In a wok, preferably nonstick, over medium-high heat, heat the oil. Add the garlic, green onions, bell peppers, and chile. Stir-fry for 1 to 2 minutes, or until fragrant and tender. Add the beans, the cumin and chili powder if using, and salt and pepper to taste. Stir-fry, tossing gently, for 1 to 2 minutes, or until heated through. Taste and adjust the seasonings.

Transfer the beans to a serving dish and spoon sour cream over them. Sprinkle with the avocado. Serve with tortilla chips and lime wedges.

TOFU AND PORK WITH CHILE-GARLIC PASTE

In many Asian markets, tofu is labeled "bean curd," a translation of its Chinese name, dou fu. It's an apt name, since tofu is made in much the same way cheese is: A starter is added to soybean "milk" to make curds, which are then pressed into blocks. This recipe calls for red chile paste flavored with garlic, which is a staple in Asian markets and is sold in some supermarkets as well.

MAKES 4 SERVINGS

2 tablespoons peanut oil

2 cloves garlic, minced

¼ pound ground lean pork

12 ounces firm tofu (bean curd), drained and cut into 1-inch cubes

1 tablespoon red chile-garlic paste

2 tablespoons soy sauce

½ teaspoon salt

¾ cup chicken broth

2 tablespoons cornstarch mixed with 3 tablespoons cold water

2 green onions, white and green parts, chopped

Heat a wok over medium-high to high heat. Pour in the oil. Add the garlic and stir-fry for a few seconds, or until fragrant. Add the pork and stir-fry for 2 to 3 minutes, or until no longer pink. Add the tofu. Stir in the chile-garlic paste, soy sauce, salt, and chicken broth. Stir in the cornstarch mixture and stir-fry for 2 minutes, or until the sauce thickens slightly.

Sprinkle with the green onions and serve immediately.

Variation: For a vegetarian dish, omit the pork and increase the amount of tofu to 1 pound. Substitute vegetable broth for the chicken broth.

TOFU WITH CHICKPEAS AND SPINACH

Chickpeas rank near the top of the nutrition charts, with an abundance of B vitamins, especially folic acid, plus iron and fiber. And research has shown that tofu and other products rich in soy protein can lower cholesterol and may help prevent some kinds of cancer. But while nutrition is great, we can give you even better reasons to eat this: It's super quick and it's tasty. To really save time, use prewashed and bagged baby spinach. Serve this dish with cooked noodles.

MAKES 4 SERVINGS

3 tablespoons vegetable oil

3 cloves garlic, minced

12 ounces extra-firm tofu, drained and cut into 1-inch cubes

½ bag (3 ounces) washed and trimmed baby spinach

1 can (15 ounces) chickpeas, rinsed and drained

¼ cup soy sauce

⅓ cup chopped fresh cilantro

Salt and freshly ground pepper

Heat a wok over medium-high to high heat. Pour in the oil. Add the garlic and stir-fry for a few seconds, or until fragrant. Add the tofu, spinach, and chickpeas and stir-fry for 2 to 3 minutes, or until hot. Stir in the soy sauce and cilantro. Season with salt and pepper to taste.

Spoon into bowls and serve immediately.

BROCCOLI WITH BROWN SUGAR

You can wrap broccoli's cabbagelike taste in a cloak of strong flavors such as garlic and hot peppers, or in a sweet sauce like this one. The vodka really perks up the sauce.

MAKES 4 SERVINGS

Sauce

3 tablespoons soy sauce

2 tablespoons firmly packed dark brown sugar

1 teaspoon cornstarch mixed with 2 tablespoons cold water

1½ tablespoons vegetable oil

2 cloves garlic, minced

2 slices fresh ginger, grated

1 pound broccoli crowns, florets separated and stems thinly sliced

2 tablespoons vodka

½ teaspoon dark sesame oil (optional)

To make the sauce: In a small bowl, whisk together the soy sauce, brown sugar, and cornstarch mixture. Set aside.

Heat a wok over medium-high to high heat. Pour in the oil. Add the garlic and ginger and stir-fry for a few seconds, or until fragrant. Stir in the broccoli and reduce the heat to medium. Cover and cook for about 4 minutes, or until the broccoli is bright green and tender-crisp.

Uncover, stir in the sauce, and stir-fry for 1 minute, or until the sauce thickens and turns clear. Sprinkle on the vodka and sesame oil, if using, and toss to mix.

Spoon the broccoli into a deep bowl and serve immediately.

ORANGE-SCENTED BABY BOK CHOY

Baby bok choy can be found in the fresh produce sections of Asian food stores as well as some supermarkets and natural food stores. It's worth seeking out. It has a striking color, which resembles jade, and a glorious, mild cabbage flavor.

MAKES 4 SERVINGS

3 tablespoons extra-virgin olive oil

1 tablespoon shredded orange zest

8 heads baby bok choy

2 tablespoons fresh orange juice

Orange slices for garnishing

In a wok over medium-low heat, heat the oil with the orange zest. Cook for 1 minute.

Increase the heat to medium-high. Add the bok choy and stir-fry for about 5 minutes, or until tender. As the bok choy cooks, drizzle it with the orange juice.

Arrange the bok choy on a platter and garnish with orange slices. Serve immediately.

MU SHU VEGETABLES

Hoisin sauce, the sweet yet spicy Asian sauce made from soybeans, was such a favorite in Barbara's family that, as a child, her daughter Dorothy was known to put it on hot dogs. This recipe is a much more traditional use for the thick brown sauce.

MAKES 4 SERVINGS

Sauce

¼ cup soy sauce

2 teaspoons cornstarch

½ teaspoon dark sesame oil

2 tablespoons peanut oil

1 teaspoon peeled, minced fresh ginger

3 cloves garlic, minced

4 cups shredded cabbage

1 cup grated carrots

2 cups fresh bean sprouts

4 warmed Asian Pancakes (page 202) or flour tortillas (see Note)

Hoisin sauce for brushing and serving

Sliced green onions for serving

To make the sauce: In a small bowl, whisk together the soy sauce, cornstarch, and sesame oil. Set aside. Stir before using.

Heat a wok over medium-high to high heat. Pour in the oil. Add the ginger and garlic and stir-fry for a few seconds, or until fragrant. Add the cabbage and stir-fry for 1 to 2 minutes, or until just tender. Mix in the carrots and bean sprouts and stir-fry for 2 to 3 minutes. Mix in the sauce and cook for about 1 minute, or until the sauce thickens and turns clear. Remove from the heat.

Set a pancake on a plate and brush it with hoisin sauce. Spread some of the hot vegetables down the center of the pancake. Fold one side over the filling, then fold in the top and bottom and roll the filled pancake to make a neat bundle. Repeat with the remaining pancakes and filling. Serve immediately with sliced green onions and additional hoisin sauce.

Note: To warm the pancakes or tortillas, wrap them in aluminum foil and place in a preheated 350°F oven for 5 to 8 minutes, or until warm.

MEDITERRANEAN VEGETABLE MEDLEY WITH CAPERS

*This is a perfect dish for late summer, but you can vary the vegetables by season.
In the spring, try asparagus, garlic, baby zucchini or baby artichokes, and spring onions. In the fall, combine
broccoli, peppers, and zucchini or eggplant. Accompany with crusty bread and a crisp green salad.*

MAKES 4 SERVINGS

2 tablespoons olive oil

5 cloves garlic, sliced

1 onion, thinly sliced

4 red, green, or yellow bell peppers, or a combination, seeded, deribbed, and cut into narrow strips

2 medium zucchini, cut into ¼-inch slices

3 tablespoons capers, including juice

2 teaspoons chopped fresh basil, or 1 teaspoon dried

Salt and freshly ground pepper

Heat a wok over medium-high to high heat. Pour in the oil. Add the garlic, onion, bell peppers, and zucchini and stir-fry for 2 to 3 minutes, or until the vegetables are tender-crisp. Stir in the capers and their juice, the basil, and salt and pepper to taste. Serve immediately.

PLANTAINS WITH MOJO FOR DIPPING

Mojo, the citrusy vinaigrette that's a staple on Cuban tables, makes a zesty counterpoint to the mild, squashlike flavor of plantains. Plantains, or "cooking bananas," are widely available in supermarkets and Latino groceries.

MAKES 4 TO 6 SERVINGS

3 large plantains

3 tablespoons vegetable oil

3 tablespoons unsalted butter

Salt

Cilantro sprigs for garnishing

Mojo (page 69) for serving

Slice the tops off the plantains and discard the tops. Cut the plantains crosswise into thirds. Using a small, sharp knife or your fingers, peel off the skin. Cut the plantains on the diagonal into ¼-inch-thick slices and set on paper towels. Using the bottom of a heavy drinking glass, flatten each slice slightly.

Heat a wok over medium-high to high heat. Pour in the oil and add the butter. Working in batches, add the plantains and stir-fry for about 2 minutes per side, or until golden brown. Using a slotted spoon, transfer to a plate.

Arrange the plantains on a serving dish, season with salt to taste, and garnish with cilantro. Serve with mojo for dipping.

BEAN THREADS WITH SHIITAKE MUSHROOMS

Also known as cellophane noodles because they're transparent, bean threads are made from the starch of mung beans, the same beans sold as bean sprouts. Reserve the shiitake stems to flavor soups or sauces.

MAKES 4 TO 6 SERVINGS

1 package (3¾ ounces) bean threads *(sai fun)*

3 tablespoons peanut oil

4 cloves garlic, minced

6 green onions, white part only, minced

10 fresh shiitake mushrooms, stemmed, caps thinly sliced

½ cup sliced water chestnuts

1 to 1½ cups diced, cooked ham, pork, or chicken, or a combination

1 cup beef broth

2 tablespoons soy sauce

Salt and freshly ground pepper

Put the bean threads in a large heatproof bowl. Add hot water to cover and soak for 15 minutes, or until softened. Drain. Using kitchen scissors, cut the noodles into shorter pieces and set aside.

In a wok, preferably nonstick, over medium-high heat, heat the oil. Add the garlic and onions and stir-fry for a few seconds, or until fragrant. Add the mushrooms, water chestnuts, and ham and stir-fry for 2 to 3 minutes, or until the mushrooms are cooked through. Add the bean threads, beef broth, and soy sauce and stir-fry for 1 to 2 minutes, or until heated through. Season with salt and pepper to taste. Let stand for a few minutes, or until all of the liquid is absorbed. Serve immediately.

PANCIT (PHILIPPINE NOODLES) WITH LIME

Pancit can be made with pork, chicken, or shrimp, or a combination. This recipe calls for rice sticks,
but thin egg noodles are a popular alternative. Pancit is also delicious garnished with thin slices of Chinese sausage.
Many thanks to Barbara's friend Dr. Myrna Paraunga for this recipe.

MAKES 4 SERVINGS

8 ounces thin rice sticks (rice vermicelli)

3 tablespoons peanut oil

2 cloves garlic, minced

1 large onion, minced

½ small head of cabbage, shredded (about 3 cups)

1 large carrot, grated

1 cup sliced celery

1 cup cooked and diced pork, chicken, or shrimp, or a combination

¼ cup fish sauce or soy sauce

1 cup chicken broth

Salt and freshly ground pepper

2 green onions, both white and green parts, chopped

1 lime, cut into wedges

Put the rice sticks in a heatproof bowl. Add hot water to cover and soak for 20 minutes, or until softened. Drain.

In a wok, preferably nonstick, over medium-high to high heat, heat the oil. Add the garlic and stir-fry for a few seconds, or until fragrant. Add the onion, cabbage, carrot, and celery. Stir-fry for 2 minutes. Add the pork, fish sauce, and broth and reduce the heat to low. When the vegetables are tender, stir in the rice sticks and season with salt and pepper to taste. Cook for 1 to 2 minutes, or until all the liquid has been absorbed by the noodles.

Transfer the noodles to a serving bowl or platter. Sprinkle with the green onions and garnish with the lime wedges. Serve immediately.

PAD THAI FOR GARLIC LOVERS

Authentic? Nah. This pad Thai, inspired by one that Virginia enjoyed in Chicago, bears little resemblance to the delicate yet spicy noodles served in many restaurants in Bangkok and the United States. But who cares? Brash and brawny, this Americanized version turns heads and wins the hearts of garlic lovers everywhere.

MAKES 4 SERVINGS

Sauce

¼ cup fish sauce

3 tablespoons sugar

2 tablespoons ketchup

7 tablespoons rice vinegar

1 to 2 teaspoons red chile paste

14 to 16 ounces rice noodles (⅛ to ¼ inch wide)

3 tablespoons peanut oil

1 to 2 tablespoons minced garlic (the more, the better)

1 cup shredded, cooked chicken breast, cooked small shrimp, or diced firm tofu, or a combination

1 Asian Omelette (page 201), cut into strips

Garnishes (your choice of)

Fresh bean sprouts

Green onions, both white and
    green parts, thinly sliced

Chopped roasted peanuts

Chopped fresh cilantro

Slivered cucumber

To make the sauce: In a bowl, whisk together the fish sauce, sugar, ketchup, vinegar, and chile paste (if you prefer, you can omit the chile paste and serve it on the side). Set aside.

Put the noodles in a large bowl. Add warm water to cover and soak for 30 minutes, or until softened. Drain.

In a wok, preferably nonstick, over medium-high heat, heat the oil. Add the garlic and stir-fry for a few seconds, or until fragrant.

Add the sauce and bring to a simmer. Add the noodles and toss to coat with the sauce. Add the chicken and omelette and cook, tossing, for about 2 minutes, or until the noodles are soft and all the ingredients are heated through. Turn the noodles out onto a platter and top with your choice of garnishes. Serve immediately.

Variation: For a vegetarian dish, omit the chicken, substitute soy sauce for the fish sauce, and use 8 ounces of diced firm tofu.

ANGEL HAIR PASTA WITH SHRIMP AND SHALLOTS

Shallots and green onions are both members of the onion family, but shallots fall a bit more on the pungent end of the scale. We love shallots and use them in a wide range of dishes. While combining shallots, garlic, and green onions in the same dish might seem like too many notes, their flavors actually create a lovely harmony.

MAKES 4 TO 6 SERVINGS

12 ounces angel hair pasta or other very thin egg noodles

2 tablespoons dark sesame oil

2 tablespoons canola oil

3 or 4 shallots, minced

2 cloves garlic, minced

1½-inch piece fresh ginger, grated

1½ pounds raw small to medium shrimp, peeled and deveined

3 bunches baby bok choy or 1 small bunch regular bok choy, cut crosswise into strips

1 bunch green onions, including both white and most of the green parts, finely chopped

1 tablespoon soy sauce

1 tablespoon unsalted butter at room temperature

Salt and freshly ground pepper

Fill a large wok, preferably nonstick, about half full of salted water and bring to a boil over high heat. Add the pasta and cook according to the package directions. Drain and transfer to a bowl. Toss with 1 tablespoon of the sesame oil. Set aside.

Dry the wok thoroughly and heat the canola oil over medium-high heat. Add the shallots, garlic, and ginger and stir-fry for a few seconds, or until fragrant. Add the shrimp and stir-fry for 1 to 2 minutes, or until opaque. Add the bok choy and green onions and stir-fry for about 1 minute, or until the bok choy is just wilted. Stir in the soy sauce, the remaining 1 tablespoon sesame oil, and the butter, then add the pasta. Cook, tossing, for 1 to 2 minutes, or until heated through. Season with salt and pepper to taste. Serve immediately.

BUCKWHEAT NOODLES WITH HOT PEANUT SAUCE

This dish is based on a Szechwan favorite that often calls for egg noodles,
but we think the earthy flavor of buckwheat stands up even better to the pungent, nutty sauce.

MAKES 4 SERVINGS

Sauce

¼ cup soy sauce

½ cup chicken broth

½ teaspoon dark sesame oil

1½ teaspoons red chile–garlic paste

4 green onions, white part only, minced

¼ cup chunky peanut butter

8 ounces thin buckwheat noodles

3 tablespoons peanut oil

2 tablespoons grated fresh ginger

3 cups shredded Chinese (napa) cabbage

1 cup grated carrots

½ cup chopped fresh cilantro

To make the sauce: In a saucepan or a small wok over medium heat, combine the soy sauce, broth, sesame oil, chile-garlic paste, green onions, and peanut butter. Heat, stirring, for 1 to 2 minutes, or until the peanut butter melts and the ingredients are well combined. Remove from the heat and set aside.

Fill a large wok, preferably nonstick, about half full of salted water and bring to a boil over high heat. Add the noodles and cook according to the package directions. Drain.

Dry the wok thoroughly and heat the oil over medium-high heat. Add the ginger and stir-fry for a few seconds, or until fragrant. Add the cabbage and carrots and stir-fry for about 3 minutes, or until the cabbage softens. Add the noodles and stir-fry for 1 to 2 minutes, or until heated through. Add the sauce and mix well.

Divide the noodles among bowls, sprinkle with the cilantro, and serve immediately.

A HILL OF NOODLES WITH GINGER

Platters of noodles accompanied by decoratively arranged meats and vegetables often are starter courses for Chinese banquets. In Chinese cuisine, noodles represent longevity and are often served for birthdays. This spicy dish makes a great centerpiece for a party. Arrange the various ingredients as attractively as you can.

MAKES 4 SERVINGS

Sauce
½ cup chicken broth

1 tablespoon soy sauce

1 tablespoon white wine

2 tablespoons grated fresh ginger

3 tablespoons red chile paste

1 tablespoon sugar

Salt and freshly ground pepper

12 ounces buckwheat noodles or thin spaghetti

3 tablespoons vegetable oil

1½ cups shredded, cooked chicken breast

1 cucumber, peeled, seeded, and thinly sliced or grated

3 eggs, lightly beaten

6 green onions, white and green parts, minced

To make the sauce: In a bowl, mix together the broth, soy sauce, wine, ginger, chile paste, sugar, and salt and pepper to taste. Set aside.

Fill a large wok, preferably nonstick, about half full of salted water and bring to a boil over high heat. Add the noodles and cook according to the package directions. Drain.

Dry the wok thoroughly and heat 2 tablespoons of the oil over medium-high heat. Add the noodles and stir-fry for 1 to 2 minutes, or until heated through. Mix in the sauce and cook for about 1 minute,

or until heated through and glossy. Transfer the noodles to a serving platter and mound them in a "hill."

Increase the heat to high, add the chicken to the wok and stir-fry for about 1 minute, or until heated through. Arrange the chicken over the noodles and top with the cucumber.

Using a paper towel, wipe the wok clean. Reheat it over medium-high heat. Pour in the remaining 1 tablespoon oil. Add the eggs and scramble. When the eggs are set, place them on top of the cucumbers on the noodle mound. Sprinkle with the green onions. Serve immediately.

RAVIOLI TOSSED WITH PANCETTA AND WALNUTS

If you're serving this dish as a main course, accompany it with a green salad and crusty country-style bread.
If you cannot find pancetta (Italian bacon), substitute top-quality domestic bacon.

MAKES 4 SERVINGS AS A FIRST COURSE / 2 AS AN ENTRÉE

1 package (9 ounces) fresh cheese ravioli

2 tablespoons extra-virgin olive oil

¼ pound pancetta, coarsely chopped

¾ cup coarsely chopped walnuts

Salt and freshly ground pepper

Freshly grated Asiago cheese for serving

Fill a large wok, preferably nonstick, about half full of salted water and bring to a boil over high heat. Add the ravioli and cook according to the package directions. Drain and set aside.

Dry the wok thoroughly. Heat the oil over medium-high heat. Add the pancetta and cook for 2 to 3 minutes, or until the pancetta begins to crisp. Add the ravioli and walnuts and cook, turning once, for 1 to 2 minutes, or until the ravioli are a pleasing golden brown. Season with salt and pepper to taste.

Spoon the ravioli onto individual plates and serve immediately. Pass the cheese at the table.

ROTINI AND DOUBLE TOMATOES WITH PINE NUTS

Who says noodles in Asian-style sauces have to be long and skinny?
Rotini (short pasta spirals) nicely "grab" the sauce in this sweet-sour medley.

MAKES 4 SERVINGS

Sauce
¼ cup bottled teriyaki sauce

2 teaspoons cornstarch

3 tablespoons rice vinegar

2 tablespoons sugar

Salt and freshly ground pepper

12 ounces rotini or other pasta of your choice

2 tablespoons peanut oil or vegetable oil

6 green onions, white part only, chopped

1 or 2 cloves garlic, minced

1 teaspoon peeled, minced fresh ginger

½ cup dried tomatoes in oil, drained and chopped

3 large fresh tomatoes, cut into wedges

8 ounces fresh snow peas or sugar snap peas

3 tablespoons pine nuts

To make the sauce: In a bowl, whisk together the teriyaki sauce, cornstarch, vinegar, sugar, and salt and pepper to taste. Set aside.

Fill a large wok, preferably nonstick, about half full of salted water and bring to a boil over high heat. Add the pasta and cook according to the package directions. Drain and set aside.

Dry the wok thoroughly and heat the oil over medium-high heat. Add the onions, garlic, and ginger and stir-fry for a few seconds, or until fragrant.

Add the dried tomatoes, fresh tomatoes, snow peas, and pine nuts. Stir-fry for about 2 minutes, or until the snow peas are bright green and the ingredients are heated through. Mix in the sauce and pasta. Stir-fry for 1 to 2 minutes, or until heated through. Serve immediately.

FARFALLE WITH RED GRAPES AND WATERCRESS

*Farfalle means "butterflies" and, with the addition of fruit, blue cheese, and peppery watercress,
this dish does take wing. A Gorgonzola dolce (Italian blue dessert cheese) is especially good in this recipe.*

MAKES 4 SERVINGS

8 ounces farfalle

1 tablespoon olive oil

3 tablespoons unsalted butter

3 cloves garlic, minced

1 red onion, cut lengthwise into 1½-inch strips

4 ounces blue cheese, crumbled

1 cup small seedless red grapes

½ bunch watercress, chopped, plus more for garnishing

Salt and freshly ground pepper

Fill a large wok, preferably nonstick, about half full of salted water and bring to a boil over high heat. Add the pasta and cook according to the package directions. Drain and set aside.

Dry the wok thoroughly. Heat the oil and butter over medium-high heat. Add the garlic and onion and stir-fry for 1 to 2 minutes, or until the onion is just tender.

Stir in the pasta, cheese, grapes, watercress, and salt and pepper to taste. Stir-fry for 1 to 2 minutes, or until the ingredients are combined and heated through.

Garnish with additional watercress and serve immediately.

CHAPTER FOUR

THE DEEP-FRYING GAME

COOKING FOODS TO A GOLDEN CRISP

WE ADMIT IT. WE LOVED TESTING RECIPES FOR THIS CHAPTER. WHAT'S NOT TO LIKE ABOUT FRIED FOODS? WHEN YOU REALLY WANT A CRISP DRUMSTICK OR A JELLY DOUGHNUT, STEAMED CHICKEN JUST DOESN'T CUT IT. FRIED FOODS ARE CRUNCHY, A TEXTURE MOST OF US FIND VERY APPEALING, AND THEY'RE RICH IN FAT, A NUTRIENT THAT, FOR CENTURIES, KEPT MANY SOCIETIES ALIVE THROUGH LEAN SEASONS AND THAT NOW ADDS INCHES TO OUR WAISTLINES. OUR ANCESTORS FRIED FOODS IN RENDERED ANIMAL FATS, BUT IN THESE NUTRITIONALLY MORE CORRECT TIMES, WE USE VEGETABLE OILS. TO BE FAIR, WE SHOULD NOTE THAT FRIED FOODS ARE OFTEN NOT AS FATTY AS FOODS THAT MAY SEEM LEANER. A FRIED CHICKEN BREAST, EVEN WITH THE SKIN, HAS LESS FAT THAN A CHEF'S SALAD WITH A QUARTER CUP OF RANCH DRESSING.

The wok and deep-frying enjoy a long history together. The typical Asian banquet table always features at least one or two fried foods to lend textural contrast to the steamed, simmered, and stir-fried fare. The wok is an excellent deep fryer because of its large surface area and ability to get very hot on the bottom. For deep-frying, you can use any heavy wok without a nonstick coating.

Like stir-frying, deep-frying is a quick cooking method. In fact, variations of many of the same guidelines for stir-frying apply to deep-frying.

GETTING READY TO FRY

Preparation is everything. Before heating up the oil, make sure all the ingredients are cut up, the batter is mixed, the seasoned flour is on a plate nearby, and a slotted spoon or tongs are within reach. Once you start cooking, you will not have time to search for ingredients or tools.

Coating foods with a batter or a dusting of cornstarch, flour, or bread crumbs helps them form a crunchy rather than a hard crust and creates a seal so the oil absorbs less of the food's flavor. Don't overdo the batter or coating, however. Batter absorbs oil like a sponge, and too much will make food taste greasy.

Starchy foods such as potatoes or potato fritters benefit from "curing"—meaning you let them sit for a while before frying. Plain potatoes often are cured in cold water, which crisps them up and removes some of the starch so they don't absorb as much oil. Letting starchy fritters and batters stand for a while helps ensure that they won't fall apart or soak up too much oil.

Before being fried, foods should be as dry as possible. If you rinse foods, pat them dry with paper towels before adding them to the oil. Moisture will make them sputter and can cause the oil to foam and smoke. Some ingredients can go directly from the freezer into the fryer, but use a long-handled utensil to slide them into the hot oil to avoid getting spattered.

Because salt causes oil to break down faster, most foods should be salted after, not before, frying. Sugar poses a different problem. Foods high in sugar, such as doughnuts, need careful watching because they can burn quickly.

PROPER TEMPERATURE IS KEY

Proper oil temperature is vital when deep-frying. If the oil is not hot enough, foods will not form a crust and will absorb more oil, making them greasy, and fritters will fall apart. If the oil gets too hot, the food will burn on the outside before the inside is cooked through. The oil also will begin to break down, giving off acrid fumes and imparting a rancid flavor to the food. When you drop foods into the oil, the temperature immediately will drop, so it's important to start with the right oil temperature (generally 350°F to 375°F) and to adjust the heat to keep the oil from cooling down or heating up too fast.

A clip-on deep-frying/candy thermometer is the best way to judge the oil temperature. Because a wok's sides are sloped, the bulb of the thermometer may touch the pan sides and give a false reading. To avoid this, fold a small piece of paper towel and wedge it tightly between the thermometer and the pan. (Do this before you heat the oil.)

Be aware of the dangers of hot oil. Keep children and pets away from the stove. Never drop foods into hot oil; instead, gently slide them in, using a spatula or a slotted spoon. If this is not possible (for example, with a dough or batter), drop the mixture gently from a spoon, holding it as close to the oil as you safely can. Before discarding the oil or straining it to reuse, let it cool down.

If you don't have a thermometer, drop a cube of white bread (trim off the crust first) into the oil, then count. If it turns golden brown in 40 seconds, the oil is about 375°F. If it takes 60 seconds to brown, the oil is about 350°F.

Don't crowd foods in the oil. Crowding makes the foods more difficult to turn and also causes the oil temperature to drop, so foods will take longer to cook and will become greasy. If each piece of food does not have room for the oil to bubble around it, the wok is too full. As a general rule, for every four cups of oil, you can fry about two-thirds of a cup of food at a time. Larger pieces of food that fry more slowly, such as cut-up chicken, can be crowded a bit more.

TIPS FOR FRYING

As with stir-frying, you need to pay attention when deep-frying. Once you drop the food into the hot oil, don't answer the phone, let the dog out, or start cleaning the kitchen counters.

How long it will take the food to brown depends on the temperature of the oil, the size of the food, whether your stove is electric or gas, and the type of wok you're using. A small bit of food, such as a mushroom, may require as little as thirty to forty seconds per side in 375°F oil. Except for larger, denser pieces such as chicken thighs, most foods will cook in less than five minutes. Be sure to turn the food as needed so it browns evenly on all sides.

To remove small pieces of food from the oil, use a slotted spoon or small strainer; use tongs for larger pieces. Then drain on paper towels. Placing a brown paper grocery bag under the paper toweling helps absorb even more grease. You can also fit a draining rack

Virginia, who until recently lived at 5,000 feet, can attest that deep-frying is one of those cooking methods noticeably affected by altitude. Foods tend to burn on the outside before they're cooked on the inside. To prevent this, lower the oil temperature by about 10 degrees and cook the food a little longer. You can also try to make foods such as fritters or doughnuts smaller than the recipe calls for. If the food has a filling, such as jelly doughnuts, it's often best to fry it without the filling. After the doughnut has cooled slightly, make a small slit in the side and use a spoon, a pastry bag, or a bulb baster to "inject" the filling.

(tempura rack) over the side of the wok. Lift the foods onto that immediately after frying to drain off some of the oil before you transfer them to paper towels. The draining rack holds only a small amount of food, so you'll need to transfer one batch to paper towels before removing the next batch from the oil.

If you have a lot of food to fry, you can keep the fried food warm in a 250°F oven while you fry the remaining batches. Some foods, such as spring rolls or potatoes, can be fried in advance, frozen, then reheated in a 325°F to 350°F oven before serving. You will lose a bit of the crispness, but when you have guests ringing the doorbell, it may be easier to turn on the oven than fire up the wok.

Better, from the standpoint of flavor and crunch, is to follow the method the professionals use: blanching. Fry the food in the oil until it's cooked through but not quite browned. Cool to room temperature, cover, and refrigerate. Pop the food into the deep fryer again just before serving, cooking it just a minute or so to nicely brown the outside.

Deep-frying does tend to smell up the house. Open some windows and turn on the exhaust fan over your stove.

TO REUSE THE OIL—OR NOT

Because you use so much oil when deep-frying, you may want to reuse it rather than throw it away. Obviously, you won't want to reuse oil in which you fried fish or onions, but in other cases, use the eye and nose test. If the oil smells OK (not acrid or rancid) and has not turned dark, it can be safely reused. Heating oil and exposing it to air reduces its smoke point (the point at which it breaks down and creates acrid fumes and "off" flavors), so oil should never be reused more than three times. We recommend reusing it only once, at most. Home cooks don't have the kind of temperature-controlled equipment found in restaurants, and it's pretty common for even fresh oil to start breaking down the first time it's used.

If the oil is still light colored and passes the "sniff test," you can clean it up to reuse later. First, use a strainer to fish out the large food particles. You can further clean the oil by adding a couple of slices of raw potato to it and heating until the potatoes turn brown. Remove the potato slices, skim the oil again, and let it cool. Line a funnel or narrow strainer with cheesecloth or a coffee filter, then carefully pour the oil through it into a clean, dry coffee can or large jar. Cover and store in a cool, dark place. Oil that has been heated is perishable. Use it within a month or toss it.

If you're going to throw out the oil, let it cool, then pour it into a can or jar without straining it. Never pour this much oil directly into the bag with the other garbage. If the bag should leak, you'll spend what seems like the rest of your life trying to get oil stains out of the carpet or your front steps.

This chapter offers a collection of some of our favorite deep-fried foods. For more fried tidbits, see the dim sum recipes in chapter 2.

USE THE RIGHT OIL

It's not just the oil temperature that's important when you deep-fry foods. You also want to use the right kind of oil. The point at which oil begins to break down and give off sharp, unpleasant fumes, a substance called acreolein, is called its smoking point. Once oil begins to break down, it can create unhealthful fumes and impart a slightly rancid flavor to foods. Some oils have higher smoking points than others, making them more suitable for frying at high temperatures.

OILS WITH SMOKING POINTS OVER 400°F
(FINE FOR DEEP-FRYING):

Avocado oil
Canola oil and canola oil blends
Corn oil
Grapeseed oil
Olive oil (pure, not extra-virgin)
Peanut oil
Sesame oil (refined)
Soybean oil
Vegetable oil (usually soybean oil)

Note: Refined sunflower and safflower oils have high smoking points but oxidize (turn rancid) easily, so we don't recommend them for deep-frying.

FATS AND OILS WITH SMOKING POINTS UNDER 400°F (BEST RESERVED FOR RAW USE OR COOKING AT LOW TEMPERATURES):

Butter
Margarine
Shortening
Extra-virgin olive oil
Dark sesame oil
Lightly refined (cold-pressed) oils of all types

Expense is also a consideration. Avocado and grapeseed oils may be wonderful for frying, but they cost a fortune. From an economic standpoint, the best all-around frying oil is vegetable (soybean) oil.

ORANGE-FLAVORED BEEF

Frying and then stir-frying the beef makes it very tender. You can easily substitute tangerine juice and zest for the orange. A garnish of sliced or chopped oranges or tangerines adds a splash of color.

MAKES 4 SERVINGS

1 pound beef flank steak, cut into very thin strips

½ cup soy sauce

Juice of 1 orange

1 tablespoon cornstarch

3 to 4 cups peanut oil

2 tablespoons rice wine vinegar

2 tablespoons oyster sauce

3 tablespoons grated orange zest

2 teaspoons grated fresh ginger

3 cloves garlic, minced

2 green onions, white part only, chopped

Fresh orange slices or tangerine segments for garnishing

In a nonreactive bowl, sprinkle the beef with ¼ cup of the soy sauce, the orange juice, and cornstarch. Toss lightly. Let stand for 30 minutes. Drain and pat dry with paper towels.

In a wok over medium-high heat, heat the oil to 375°F. Reduce the heat to medium. Add the beef, about ½ cup at a time, separating the strips as you slide them into the hot oil. Blanch the beef for a few seconds, or until no longer pink. Using a slotted spoon, remove the beef and drain on paper towels. Set the beef aside. Let the oil in the wok cool.

In a small bowl, mix the remaining ¼ cup soy sauce with the vinegar and oyster sauce. Set aside.

Remove all but 1 tablespoon of the cooled oil from the wok and reheat the wok over medium-high heat. Add the orange zest, ginger, garlic, and green onions. Stir-fry for about 1 minute, or until fragrant. Add the beef and stir-fry for about 2 minutes, or until cooked through. Add the oyster sauce mixture and cook for 1 to 2 minutes, or until heated through.

Mound on a serving plate, garnish with orange slices, and serve immediately.

CLASSIC FRIED CHICKEN

Some Southern cooks like to soak their chicken in salt water before frying. Back in the days when most chickens came from the backyard, this helped rid them of any gamy flavor. This step still serves a purpose now that most of us buy our chicken in plastic-wrapped packages from the supermarket—it helps crisp the skin and flavor the bird.

MAKES 4 TO 6 SERVINGS

6 cups cold water

1 tablespoon salt, plus more as needed

2½ to 3 pounds chicken breasts, thighs, or drumsticks, or a combination

4 to 5 cups vegetable oil or corn oil

1 cup all-purpose flour

½ teaspoon paprika

1 teaspoon poultry seasoning, or mixed dried herbs

Freshly ground pepper

In a large bowl, combine the cold water and the 1 tablespoon salt, stirring to dissolve the salt. Put the chicken pieces in the bowl, making sure they are covered with the water. Refrigerate for at least 3 hours or up to 12 hours.

In a wok over medium-high heat, heat the oil to 375°F.

Meanwhile, on a plate, mix the flour with the paprika, poultry seasoning, and pepper to taste. Drain the chicken pieces and pat dry with paper towels. Dredge lightly in the flour mixture, shaking off excess.

Reduce the heat to medium and slide the chicken thighs and drumsticks into the hot oil. Fry, turning once with tongs, for 3 minutes. Add the chicken breasts, carefully rearranging the chicken to fit all the pieces. To make more room in the wok, you can "prop" the drumsticks so the skinny parts rest against the sides of the wok. Or, fry the chicken in batches.

Fry, turning the chicken occasionally and adjusting the heat as needed to keep the oil between 350°F and 375°F, for 12 to 15 minutes more, or until golden and cooked through. (Cut into a piece to test.)

Using tongs, remove the chicken and drain on paper towels. Season lightly with salt if desired. Serve warm or cold.

VERY LEMONY CHICKEN

Marinating the chicken in lemon juice nicely tenderizes it. The citrusy sauce is drizzled on both the lettuce and the chicken, making the lettuce an important part of the dish, rather than just a garnish.

MAKES 4 TO 6 SERVINGS

4 boneless, skinless chicken breast halves (about 1 pound)

1 cup fresh lemon juice

Sauce

1½ cups water

½ cup fresh lemon juice

3 tablespoons firmly packed light brown sugar

3 tablespoons cornstarch

3 tablespoons honey

1 tablespoon chicken broth

2 teaspoons peeled, minced fresh ginger

1 lemon, cut into thin slices

Batter

¾ cup cornstarch

1 teaspoon baking powder

1 teaspoon garlic powder

½ teaspoon salt

¼ teaspoon freshly ground pepper

¼ cup water

2 eggs, lightly beaten

3 to 4 cups vegetable oil

6 cups shredded iceberg or romaine lettuce

In a nonreactive bowl, cover the chicken with the 1 cup lemon juice. Refrigerate for 4 to 6 hours. Drain.

To make the sauce: In a small saucepan or nonstick wok over medium heat, combine the water, ½ cup lemon juice, brown sugar, cornstarch, honey, chicken broth, and ginger. Cook, stirring constantly, for about 5 minutes, or until the sauce thickens and turns clear. Stir in the lemon slices. Remove from the heat and set aside. Reheat just before serving.

To make the batter: In a bowl, whisk together the cornstarch, baking powder, garlic powder, salt, pepper, water, and eggs.

In a wok over medium-high heat, heat the oil to 375°F. Reduce the heat to medium. Working with 2 chicken breast halves at a time, dip each one into the batter, then slide, one at a time, into the hot oil. Fry for 8 to 10 minutes, or until golden brown on each side. Using tongs, remove the chicken and drain on paper towels. Place the chicken on a cutting board and cut into ½-inch slices.

To serve, spread the lettuce on a serving plate and arrange the hot chicken on top. Pour the lemon sauce over and serve immediately.

PUB FISH-AND-CHIPS

English pubs traditionally serve fish-and-chips (what we Yanks call French fries) in cones formed from newspaper. That's a great way to recycle newspapers, but we prefer a somewhat cleaner wrapping of parchment paper. Of course, you can just serve the fish-and-chips on a plate. Plaice is the fish traditionally used for fish-and-chips, but it's hard to find in the States, so we substitute flounder or sole. If you like your potatoes extra-crispy, fry them once at 350°F, and then again at 375°F just before serving. Don't forget to wash it all down with a good English ale.

MAKES 4 SERVINGS

Batter
¾ cup all-purpose flour
1 egg, separated
½ cup English ale, or cold water

4 or 5 baking potatoes (about 1½ pounds total), scrubbed
3 to 4 cups vegetable or canola oil
1 to 1¼ pounds flounder or sole fillets, or other thin white fish
Salt
Four 12-inch square pieces of parchment paper or newspaper
Malt vinegar for serving

To make the batter: Put the flour in a bowl. In a separate bowl, combine the egg yolk and ale. Pour the egg mixture into the flour, stirring until the batter is smooth. Let stand for 20 minutes. Stir before using.

Cut the potatoes into wedges slightly more than ⅛ inch thick. Put them in a large bowl of ice water and let stand for 20 minutes, then drain and pat dry with paper towels.

In a clean bowl, beat the egg white to stiff, glossy peaks.

In a wok over medium-high heat, heat the oil to 375°F. Fold the egg white into the batter. Dip the fish into the batter, then slide carefully into the hot oil. Fry for about 2 minutes per side, or until golden brown. Using tongs, remove the fish and drain on paper towels. Season with salt to taste. If necessary, keep the fish warm in a 300°F oven.

Working in small batches, fry the potatoes for 2 to 4 minutes, or until tender and golden brown. Using a slotted spoon, remove the potatoes and drain on paper towels. Season with salt to taste.

To serve, arrange a fish fillet and one fourth of the potatoes in the center of a sheet of parchment paper. Roll the paper in a cone shape and fold over the bottom piece. Repeat with the remaining fish and potatoes. Serve hot with malt vinegar.

BUTTERFLIED SHRIMP WITH WALNUTS

Don't be overwhelmed when you see an Asian recipe with multiple steps. If you do these small steps separately, you'll find the recipes are not difficult. For example, make the sauce and batter ahead of time and refrigerate them. If the batter thickens, add a little water. The shrimp can be butterflied in advance and refrigerated. Then it's just a matter of assembling the dish and quickly cooking it.

MAKES 4 SERVINGS

Sauce

½ cup white wine vinegar

½ cup sugar

¼ cup pineapple juice

5 tablespoons ketchup

2 teaspoons cornstarch mixed with 2 tablespoons cold water

Batter

½ cup all-purpose flour

¼ cup water

1 egg, lightly beaten

3 tablespoons dry white wine

1 pound raw extra-large shrimp, peeled and deveined

2 to 3 cups peanut oil

4 cups shredded iceberg lettuce

⅓ cup walnuts, preferably toasted (see page 209)

To make the sauce: In a small wok or saucepan over medium-low heat, combine the vinegar, sugar, pineapple juice, and ketchup. Heat until the sauce begins to boil. Stir in the cornstarch mixture and continue cooking until the sauce thickens and turns clear. Remove from the heat and set aside. Reheat just before serving.

To make the batter: In a bowl, whisk together the flour, water, egg, and wine. Let stand for 20 minutes. Stir before using.

Using a small, sharp knife, cut lengthwise almost all the way through each shrimp. Flatten the shrimp slightly. Pat dry with paper towels.

In a wok over medium-high heat, heat the oil to 375°F. Working with 6 or 7 shrimp at a time, dip each one into the batter, then slide into the hot oil. Fry for 1 to 2 minutes, or until golden brown. Using a slotted spoon, remove the shrimp and drain on paper towels.

To serve, spread the lettuce on a serving plate and arrange the shrimp on top. Drizzle with the sauce and sprinkle with the walnuts. Serve immediately.

OYSTER AND VEGETABLE TEMPURA

Shrimp and fish are commonly found on tempura platters in Japanese restaurants, but oysters are also excellent fried in tempura batter. The secret to a good tempura is the thin, cold batter. It "explodes" in the hot oil, forming a light, crunchy coating. You can vary the vegetables according to the season and your taste. If you have access to an Asian market, use fresh lotus root (see page 212), cut crosswise into thin slices.

MAKES 4 SERVINGS

Batter

1 cup cake flour or glutinous rice flour (see Note)

¼ teaspoon salt

1 jumbo egg yolk

1 tablespoon mirin or dry white wine

¾ to 1 cup very cold water

Vegetables (Choose 2 or 3)

2 green or red bell peppers, seeded, deribbed, and cut into squarish pieces

4 ounces green beans

2 ounces sugar snap peas

8 asparagus spears, cut into 2-inch pieces

1 cup broccoli florets

4 green onions, both white and green parts, each cut crosswise into 3 pieces

1 medium sweet potato, partially cooked, then peeled and cut into ¼-inch slices

8 baby carrots, halved lengthwise

1 Japanese eggplant (4 to 5 ounces), thinly sliced

Cake flour or glutinous rice flour for dusting

4 cups corn, vegetable, or canola oil

12 shucked oysters, drained and patted dry

Sweet Soy Dipping Sauce (page 204), preferably made with dashi, for serving

To make the batter: In a bowl, whisk together the flour, salt, egg yolk, mirin, and water. You will need ⅞ to 1 cup water if using cake flour, ¾ to ⅞ cup if using rice flour. The batter will be very thin. Do not overmix. Use immediately, or cover and refrigerate for up to 1 hour. Stir before using.

To prepare the vegetables: Pat the vegetables dry with paper towels. Using a little flour, lightly dust the smooth, slippery vegetables such as sugar snap peas and asparagus (this helps the batter to adhere). Set aside.

In a wok over medium-high heat, heat the oil to 375ºF. Reduce the heat to medium.

Working in batches, dip the vegetables into the batter, letting excess batter drain off, then slide into the hot oil. Fry for 1 to 2 minutes, or until the batter is a light golden brown and very crisp. Pieces of the batter will break off; skim them out of the oil frequently. Using a slotted spoon, remove the vegetables and drain on paper towels.

Working with 4 to 6 oysters at a time, dip each one into the batter, then slide into the hot oil. Fry for 1 to 2 minutes per side, or until golden. Using a slotted spoon, remove the oysters and drain on paper towels.

Serve immediately with the dipping sauce.

Note: Do not use all-purpose flour in this recipe. It contains too much gluten (the protein that makes bread chewy) and will not produce the extra-crunchy coating. Glutinous rice flour, available in Asian markets, makes a light, crunchy restaurant-style tempura, but the more readily available cake flour works fine, too.

CHILES RELLENOS CON QUESO

*A Mexican favorite, this dish plays the spiciness of the chiles against the richness of the cheese.
Serve with refried beans and rice.*

MAKES 4 SERVINGS AS AN APPETIZER / 2 AS AN ENTRÉE

Salsa

2 tablespoons vegetable oil

1 medium onion, chopped

3 cloves garlic, minced

3 red bell peppers, seeded, deribbed, and chopped

¼ cup tomato purée

½ teaspoon ground cumin

Salt and freshly ground pepper

Batter

¾ cup all-purpose flour, sifted

½ cup milk

1 teaspoon vegetable oil

1 egg, lightly beaten

¼ teaspoon salt

8 long, slender, mild green chiles, such as poblano

8 ounces mild Cheddar cheese, cut into small pieces

3 tablespoons minced onion

3 to 4 cups vegetable oil

To make the salsa: In a small wok or saucepan over medium heat, heat the oil. Add the onion and garlic and cook for a few seconds, or until fragrant. Add the bell peppers and cook for 3 to 4 minutes, or until tender. Add the tomato purée, cumin, and salt and pepper to taste. Simmer for 1 minute. Taste and adjust the seasonings. Remove from the heat and set aside. Reheat before serving.

To make the batter: In a bowl, whisk together the flour, milk, oil, egg, and salt. Let stand for 20 minutes. Stir before using.

Using a small, sharp knife, make a small slit below the stem of each chile and remove the seeds. Stuff some of the cheese and onion into each chile, being careful not to open the chile more than is necessary.

In a wok over medium-high heat, heat the oil to 375ºF. Pour the batter into a shallow dish. Working with 3 chiles at a time, roll each one in the batter, then slide into the hot oil. Fry, turning once, for about 2 minutes per side, or until golden brown. Using a slotted spoon, remove the chiles and drain on paper towels.

Place 2 to 4 chiles on each plate and serve hot with the salsa.

INDIAN-STYLE POTATO FRITTERS

Vegetable fritters of various kinds are a staple in India, a largely vegetarian country. Be sure to let the fritters chill before frying them to help keep them from falling apart. Tangy raita, the classic Indian yogurt dip, complements the fritters nicely. But you can serve them with plain yogurt or mango chutney instead.

MAKES 12 TO 14 FRITTERS

Raita (Yogurt Sauce)

1 cup finely chopped cucumber

½ teaspoon salt

1 cup plain yogurt

¼ cup chopped fresh cilantro

Fritters

3 large baking potatoes (about 2½ pounds total)

2 tablespoons vegetable oil

1 cup finely chopped onion

1 teaspoon garam masala, or best-quality curry powder

½ teaspoon ground coriander

¼ to ½ teaspoon cayenne pepper

1 teaspoon black mustard seeds (optional)

2 tablespoons fresh lemon juice

1 teaspoon salt

½ cup flour, preferably whole wheat

3 to 4 cups vegetable oil

To make the raita: Sprinkle the cucumber with the salt and put in a colander to drain for at least 30 minutes. In a bowl, combine the cucumber with the yogurt and cilantro. Stir well, cover, and refrigerate until ready to serve.

To make the fritters: Pierce the potatoes in 2 or 3 places and place, thick ends facing out, in a circle in the microwave. Microwave on high, turning once, for 10 to 15 minutes, or until the potatoes can be easily pierced with a fork. Or preheat a conventional oven to 375ºF and bake the potatoes for 45 to 50 minutes, or until they can be easily pierced with a fork. Let stand until cool enough to handle, then peel. (To peel the potatoes, place them on a cutting board and smash them with the back of your hand. The peel and flesh will easily separate.)

Meanwhile, heat a wok or large skillet over medium-high heat. Pour in the oil. Add the onion, garam masala, coriander, cayenne pepper to taste, and mustard seeds (if using). Cook, stirring frequently, for 1 to 2 minutes, or until the spices smell very fragrant and the mustard seeds begin to pop. Remove from the heat and set aside.

Add the peeled potatoes to the spice mixture. Add the lemon juice and salt and stir, using the back of a spoon to break up and mash the potatoes.

Line a plate or baking sheet with waxed paper. Put the flour in a shallow dish. With lightly oiled hands, form the potato mixture into patties, each about 2 inches in diameter and ½ inch thick. You should have 12 to 14 fritters. Roll them in the flour, then place on the prepared plate or baking sheet. Cover with plastic wrap and refrigerate for at least 20 minutes or up to 24 hours.

In a wok over medium-high heat, heat the oil to 375ºF. Slide the fritters, 3 or 4 at a time, into the hot oil and fry, turning once, for 2 to 4 minutes, or until golden. Using a slotted spoon or spatula, remove the fritters and drain on paper towels.

Serve warm with the raita.

Note: If the fritters start to fall apart, the oil has cooled down too much. Let it heat to 375ºF before adding more fritters.

FRIED MUSHROOMS IN BEER BATTER

Beer is a popular ingredient in batters for deep-frying. It adds both flavor and lightness, thanks to the malt and yeasts it contains. Accompany the fried mushrooms with cold beer.

MAKES 4 TO 6 SERVINGS

Batter

½ cup cornstarch

½ cup all-purpose flour

2 eggs, beaten

¾ cup light beer

1 tablespoon poppy seeds

12 ounces fresh oyster or shiitake mushrooms

3 cups vegetable oil

To make the batter: In a bowl, whisk together the cornstarch, flour, eggs, beer, and poppy seeds. Let stand for 20 minutes. Stir before using.

If using shiitake mushrooms, remove the stems and discard.

In a wok over medium-high heat, heat the oil to 375ºF. Working with about 6 mushrooms at a time, dip each one into the batter, then slide into the hot oil. Fry for 1 to 2 minutes, or until golden. Using a slotted spoon, remove the mushrooms and drain on paper towels. Serve hot.

NORTHERN GREEK–STYLE ZUCCHINI WITH TZATZIKI

Barbara's daughter Reba, who lives in Solonika, Greece, always contributes one recipe to each of Barbara's cookbooks. This Greek-style fried zucchini is Reba's recipe, a winner as usual. It tastes great with a Greek salad of cucumbers and tomatoes dressed lightly with olive oil and vinegar. Prepare the tzatziki the day before serving.

MAKES 4 SERVINGS

Tzatziki

3 cups plain yogurt

4 cloves garlic, minced

½ cup seeded, grated cucumber (optional)

¼ cup chopped fresh dillweed, or 2 tablespoons dried dillweed (optional)

12 baby zucchini (each 3 to 4 inches long), halved lengthwise

4 eggs, lightly beaten

1 cup all-purpose flour

¼ teaspoon dried oregano, or to taste

Salt and freshly ground pepper

3 cups vegetable oil

To make the tzatziki: Line a small colander or strainer with a double thickness of cheesecloth. Set the colander over a bowl. Spoon the yogurt into the colander. (This step is optional but allows the liquid to drain off, thickening the yogurt.) Cover loosely with plastic wrap and refrigerate for 2 hours. Discard accumulated liquid. Spoon the yogurt into a bowl. Mix in the garlic and cucumber and dill, if using. Cover and refrigerate until ready to serve. Stir before serving.

Put the zucchini in a bowl of salted cold water and let stand for 20 minutes. Drain and pat dry with paper towels.

Pour the eggs into a shallow bowl. On a plate, combine the flour with the oregano and salt and pepper to taste.

In a wok over medium-high heat, heat the oil to 375°F. Working in batches, roll each piece of zucchini in the eggs, letting the excess drip off, then roll in the flour mixture. Slide the zucchini into the hot oil and fry, turning, for about 2 minutes, or until golden brown and tender but not mushy. Using a slotted spoon, remove the zucchini and drain on paper towels.

Serve the zucchini hot with the tzatziki.

SWEET POTATO FRIES WITH KETCHUP

Double-frying makes French fries extra crispy. Leaving the skin on the sweet potatoes retains more flavor and vitamins. If you prefer white potatoes, substitute russets and proceed as directed. You can also combine russet and sweet potatoes.

MAKES 4 TO 6 SERVINGS

1½ pounds sweet potatoes or yams, scrubbed

6 cups vegetable oil

Salt

Crushed dried rosemary for sprinkling

Spicy Ketchup (page 206) or store-bought ketchup for serving

Cut the sweet potatoes in half crosswise, then lengthwise into slices about ¼ inch thick. Put them in a large bowl of ice water and let stand for 15 minutes. Drain and pat dry, in small batches, with paper towels.

Line 2 baking sheets with paper towels. In a wok over medium-high heat, heat the oil to 350°F. Using a large slotted spoon, carefully lower a few of the potato slices into the hot oil. Fry for 4 to 5 minutes, or until tender and lightly browned.

Using the slotted spoon, remove the potatoes and drain on the prepared baking sheet. At this point, the potatoes can stand at room temperature for up to 2 hours.

Just before serving, reheat the oil over medium-high heat to 375°F. Using the slotted spoon, carefully lower a few of the potato slices into the hot oil. Fry for 2 to 3 minutes, or until golden brown. Using a slotted spoon, remove the potatoes and drain on paper towels. Sprinkle the potatoes with salt and rosemary to taste. Serve hot with ketchup.

JELLY DOUGHNUTS

Jelly doughnuts are called Berliners in New England, and Barbara has fond childhood memories of these sugary treats with their jewel-like fillings. Invite some friends over because these don't keep well. You can make larger doughnuts by using a 3½- to 4-inch cookie cutter.

MAKES ABOUT 20 TO 22 DOUGHNUTS

1 package fast-rising yeast

1 cup lukewarm milk (105°F to 110°F)

¼ cup sugar, plus more for rolling

3½ cups all-purpose flour

½ teaspoon salt

4 tablespoons unsalted butter, melted and cooled

3 eggs; 1 separated, white lightly beaten

1 teaspoon vanilla extract

Raspberry, strawberry, or apricot jelly or jam, or a combination

4 cups vegetable oil

In a bowl, stir together the yeast, ¼ cup of the milk, and 1 teaspoon of the sugar. Let stand in a warm, draft-free area for 5 minutes, or until bubbly.

Meanwhile, sift the flour, the remaining sugar, and the salt into the large bowl of an electric mixer fitted with the dough hook (or use a bowl and a wooden spoon). Add the butter, the remaining ¾ cup milk, the eggs, egg yolk, and vanilla. Add the yeast mixture and beat on medium speed or stir for 2 to 3 minutes, or until a soft dough forms. Gather the dough into a ball and place on a floured pastry cloth. Knead the dough for 1 to 2 minutes, to form a soft but not sticky dough. Shape it into a ball and place in a lightly greased bowl. Cover with a hot, damp towel and let stand in a warm, draft-free area for about 1 hour, or until it doubles in bulk. Punch down the dough

On a lightly floured pastry cloth, roll out the dough to ¼- to ½-inch thickness. Cut out circles with a 2½- to 3-inch cookie cutter. Using a pastry brush, brush the edges of one circle with the beaten egg white.

Spoon 1 teaspoon jelly in the center. Place another dough circle on top and pinch the edges firmly together, sealing the 2 rounds. Repeat with the remaining dough circles. Arrange the doughnuts, on a floured plate or baking sheet. Let rise in a warm, draft-free area for about 30 minutes, or until light.

In a wok over medium-high heat, heat the oil to 375°F. Carefully slide the doughnuts, a few at a time, into the hot oil and fry for 1 to 2 minutes, or until golden brown on one side. Carefully turn them over and fry for about 2 minutes, or until golden brown on the other side. They brown quickly; watch carefully so they do not burn. Using a slotted spoon, remove the doughnuts and drain on paper towels.

Spread sugar on a plate and while the doughnuts are still very warm, roll them in the sugar. Let cool. These are good slightly warm or at room temperature but should be served the same day they are made.

BEIGNETS

*These sweet, eggy French-style puffs drenched in confectioners' sugar are one of New Orleans'
famous tourist attractions. They're messy to eat, but that's a lot of their charm. If you really want to gild the lily,
drizzle these with chocolate sauce just before serving.*

MAKES 20 BEIGNETS

1 cup water

2 tablespoons granulated sugar

¼ teaspoon salt

4 tablespoons unsalted butter

⅛ teaspoon freshly grated nutmeg

1¼ cups all-purpose flour, sifted

4 eggs

1 teaspoon vanilla extract

3 cups vegetable oil

Confectioners' sugar for dusting

In a nonstick wok or medium-large saucepan over medium heat, mix together the water, granulated sugar, salt, butter, and nutmeg. Bring to a boil, then remove the wok from the heat. Using a wooden spoon, stir in the flour, mixing until all of it is incorporated. Set the wok over medium heat and cook, beating continuously, until the dough forms a ball and pulls away from the sides of the pan. Remove from the heat. Transfer the batter to the large bowl of an electric mixer fitted with the dough hook and let cool slightly. Add the eggs, one at a time, beating well on medium speed after each addition. The mixture should be smooth and shiny. Mix in the vanilla.

Clean the wok and dry thoroughly. Pour in the oil and heat over medium-high heat to 375°F. Using a tablespoon, scoop out a rounded spoonful of batter, then use another spoon to release the batter and slide it into the hot oil. Fry 5 or 6 beignets at a time for 3 to 4 minutes, or until golden brown on all sides. Using a slotted spoon, remove the beignets and drain on paper towels.

Sprinkle the beignets generously with confectioners' sugar. Arrange on a serving dish or on individual plates and serve warm.

FRIED BISCUITS WITH APPLE BUTTER

Bring these crunchy biscuits to the table piping hot. While homemade apple butter is lovely, you can serve them with store-bought apple butter, pumpkin butter, or strawberry jam instead.

MAKES ABOUT 16 BISCUITS

¼ cup lukewarm water (105ºF to 110ºF)

½ teaspoon honey

1 package fast-rising yeast

1 cup milk

⅓ cup vegetable shortening, cut into ½-inch pieces

3½ cups all-purpose flour

½ teaspoon salt

3 cups vegetable oil

Apple Butter (recipe follows) for serving

In a small bowl, combine the water and honey. Add the yeast and stir to dissolve. Let stand in a warm, draft-free area for 5 to 10 minutes, or until bubbly.

In a small wok or saucepan over medium heat, combine the milk and shortening and heat for 3 to 4 minutes, or until the milk is very hot and the shortening is melting. Cool to lukewarm.

Meanwhile, in the large bowl of an electric mixer fitted with the dough hook, stir together the flour and salt. Add the yeast mixture and the milk-shortening mixture and beat on medium speed for 3 to 4 minutes, or until a sticky dough forms. Turn the dough out onto a lightly floured pastry cloth and knead for about 2 minutes, or until smooth. Shape it into a ball and place in a greased bowl.

Cover loosely and let stand in a warm, draft-free area for about 1 hour, or until it doubles in bulk. Punch down the dough.

On a lightly floured pastry cloth, roll out the dough to ½- to ¾-inch thickness. Cut out circles with a 3-inch cookie cutter.

In a wok over medium-high heat, heat the oil to 375ºF. Carefully slide the biscuits, 4 or 5 at a time, into the hot oil and fry for about 3 minutes, or until golden brown on one side. Turn them over and fry for 3 minutes, or until golden brown on the other side. Using a slotted spoon, remove the biscuits and drain on paper towels.

Serve immediately with apple butter.

APPLE BUTTER

Apple butter makes a great gift for friends or relatives. Use a cooking or all-purpose apple such as Jonathan, Northern Spy, Stayman, Rome Beauty, or Winesap. This recipe works best in a nonstick wok.

MAKES ABOUT 2 CUPS

3 pounds tart cooking apples, peeled, cored, and thinly sliced

⅔ cup apple juice

2¼ cups sugar

2 tablespoons ground cinnamon

½ teaspoon freshly grated nutmeg

¼ teaspoon ground cloves

1 teaspoon vanilla extract

3 tablespoons unsalted butter

In a nonstick wok, toss the apples with the apple juice, sugar, cinnamon, nutmeg, cloves, vanilla, and butter. Bring to a simmer over medium-low heat and cook, stirring occasionally, for about 45 minutes, or until the apples are soft.

Transfer the mixture to a bowl and mash the apples with a spoon, or process in a food processor fitted with the steel blade. Return the apple mixture to the wok. Bring to a simmer over medium-low heat and cook, stirring occasionally, for 35 to 40 minutes, or until the mixture is smooth and thick. Taste and adjust the seasonings as needed.

Ladle the apple butter into hot sterilized jars and seal and process according to the manufacturer's directions for jellies and jams. Let cool, then store at cool room temperature. Or, spoon the apple butter into a bowl, cover, refrigerate, and use within a few days. Stir before serving.

CHAPTER FIVE

STEAM HEAT

COOKING OVER LIQUID

IF DEEP-FRYING IS THOUGHT OF AS "BAD" FOR YOU, STEAMING HAS THE OPPOSITE REPUTATION. PERHAPS BECAUSE OF THAT STEAMED VEGETABLE PLATE TOO MANY RESTAURANTS STILL SERVE TO DINERS WHO ASK FOR A VEGETARIAN MEAL, STEAMING BRINGS TO MIND FOOD THAT'S HEALTHFUL BUT ALSO BLAND TO THE POINT OF BEING BORING. ⌣ NOTHING COULD BE FURTHER FROM THE TRUTH. WHILE STEAMING IS INDEED A GREAT WAY TO COOK VEGETABLES AND IS NOT THE BEST WAY TO COOK, SAY, A T-BONE STEAK, IT IS A VERSATILE COOKING METHOD. YOU CAN STEAM A WIDE VARIETY OF FOODS, INCLUDING SOME MEATS AND EVEN DESSERTS, SUCH AS AN OUT-OF-THIS-WORLD WHITE CHOCOLATE BREAD PUDDING.

We don't mean to downplay the health benefits of steaming. When fruits, vegetables, and grains are steamed rather than boiled, they retain up to one-third more of their water-soluble vitamins (such as vitamin C and folate). Steaming is also a no-fat cooking method because you need not add any fat.

Steaming is both gentle and invigorating—the equivalent of a sauna for food. When steamed, foods retain flavor, moisture, and texture. It's an especially good way to cook foods that you want to keep a "clean" flavor, such as fish, shellfish, dumplings, and vegetables. It also maintains a moist texture in foods such as dense cakes that lean more toward puddings, and in eggs and egg-based foods that benefit from gentle heat. Steaming is an excellent way to reheat cooked foods such as rice without drying them out.

Health and flavor are not the only reasons to steam. Tradition plays a big role. Steamers date back at least 3,000 years in China, where steaming is still one of the ways the wok is used most frequently. The wok is great for steaming because of its broad diameter. It's roomy enough to accommodate most foods in a single layer, so they steam quickly and evenly. In China, even breads often are steamed, because the traditional Chinese kitchen lacks an oven. In Europe, steaming is used to cook dense puddings (more like what Americans would call cakes), including the predecessor to the baked fruitcake. An American survivor is Boston brown bread.

Steaming is fast and easy. Unlike stir-frying and deep-frying, it's a hands-off method. Just put the food in a bamboo steamer or on a steamer tray, cover the wok, and leave it alone. Except for one quick peek to make sure the water level hasn't gone down too far (for foods that steam ten minutes or longer), keep the wok covered so steam does not escape and increase the total cooking time.

TYPES OF STEAMERS

The traditional steamer used with a wok is woven of bamboo. The steamer sits in the wok and is covered with its own lid. Because bamboo is porous, condensation can escape so water doesn't drip back on the food. Bamboo steamers are roomy, inexpensive, and easy to handle because they don't get too hot. They stack easily and, if you buy a steamer with two compartments, you can steam a big batch of dumplings all at once. Because bamboo steamers absorb odors and oils, put the food on a plate or on lettuce leaves or foil rather than directly on the steamer bottom.

A steamer rack is also widely used with woks. The rack is either a metal rimmed plate with holes punched into it or a round wire grid that fits in the wok. You can oil the rack and put the food directly on it or, for more gentle indirect steaming, put the food on a plate and set the plate on the rack. Then cover both the steamer and the wok with the wok lid.

If you don't have a steamer, you can make your own: Place a heatproof cup (a glass baking cup is perfect) upside down in the wok and set a heatproof plate atop it. Instead of using a heatproof cup, you can wedge two chopsticks in the wok, then top with two more chopsticks going the other direction. Make sure they fit tightly enough so they won't collapse, then set a plate atop them.

STEAMING TIPS

It's especially important to shop wisely for ingredients when steaming because this cooking method enhances the flavors of foods. Select the very best fruits, vegetables, chicken, and fish. If you want to try steaming meats, choose tender cuts. Save the tougher cuts for braising (see chapter 6).

It's best to steam foods in a single layer with enough space between them for the steam to circulate. If you plan to steam large batches of food, invest in a two-tiered bamboo steamer. (The foods in the upper tier may take a few minutes longer to cook.)

The water should come high enough in the wok so it will generate plenty of steam and not boil away, but not actually touch the food. Fill the wok one-half to two-thirds full of water. The food should be at least an inch above the liquid. To add a subtle flavor to steamed foods, you can add aromatics such as orange or lemon zest, lemongrass, spices, or herbs to the steaming water.

Bring the water to a boil over high heat, then reduce the heat to medium. For foods that steam longer than ten minutes, check the water once, about halfway through the steaming time, to make sure the water level hasn't gone down too much. Other than that one peek, do not uncover the wok during steaming, or you'll let steam escape, increasing the cooking time. If the wok lid is bent and a fair amount of steam is escaping, wrap a damp paper towel around the rim of the wok where it meets the lid.

If you're steaming foods in containers (such as custard cups), lay a sheet of waxed paper or foil over the cups to keep moisture from dripping back into the food.

When uncovering the wok or steamer, be careful not to get your hands or face too close to the steam wafting out of the pan.

You'll also find several excellent steamed dim sum tidbits in chapter 2. For tips on making perfect steamed rice, see page 203.

SWORDFISH MARGARITA WITH PAPAYA SALSA

Cultures around the world steam foods in leaf-wrapped bundles, and the Americas are no exception.
This dish borrows the summery, lime-kissed flavor of a margarita to give swordfish a boost.
Obviously, corn on the cob would be a great side dish with this recipe.

MAKES 4 SERVINGS

Salsa

2 cups peeled, seeded, and diced papaya (from 1 small to medium papaya)

½ cup finely chopped fresh cilantro

1 small red onion, chopped

1 orange or green bell pepper, seeded, deribbed, and chopped

3 tablespoons fresh lime juice

⅛ teaspoon red pepper flakes

Marinade

1 cup fresh lime juice

2 tablespoons tequila

¼ teaspoon salt

1½ pounds swordfish, cut into 4 pieces

8 fresh corn husks (the outermost green leaves), soaked in water 15 minutes and drained

To make the salsa: In a small nonreactive bowl, combine the papaya, cilantro, onion, bell pepper, lime juice, and red pepper flakes and toss to mix. Cover loosely and refrigerate until ready to serve. Just before serving, toss the salsa again, taste, and adjust the seasonings.

To make the marinade: In a small bowl, combine the lime juice, tequila, and salt. Place the fish in a large, self-sealing plastic bag and add the marinade. Seal the bag tightly and turn it several times so the fish is coated by the marinade. Set the bag in a shallow dish and refrigerate for 2 hours, turning once. Drain the fish and discard the marinade.

Place a piece of fish in the natural curve of a corn husk and cover it with another corn husk. Turn the ends under, making a neat package, tamale style. Tie the husks together with kitchen string or long chives. Repeat with the remaining fish and corn husks.

Fill a wok one-half to two-thirds full of water and bring to a boil over high heat. Reduce the heat to medium and fit an oiled steamer rack or bamboo steamer in the wok. If using a bamboo steamer, set an oiled heat-proof plate in it. Arrange the fish packages on the rack or plate. Cover and steam for 8 to 12 minutes, or until the fish is slightly firm to the touch and flakes easily when prodded gently with a fork. You will have to open one of the packages to check.

Using a slotted spoon, transfer the fish packages to individual plates. Allow diners to open their own packages. Serve immediately with the salsa.

You can steam corn at the same time you steam the fish. Remove the husks and silk from the corn. Set the corn around the fish or, if you have a double-tiered steamer, place the corn in the top tier. Cover the steamer with a tight-fitting lid and steam for 8 to 10 minutes. Serve the corn alongside the fish, and pass butter and salt at the table.

GINGERED CHICKEN AND EDAMAME

Edamame, or fresh green soybeans, have grown in popularity in the last few years (see page 212). They can be found in natural-foods stores, Asian markets, and some supermarkets, either fresh or frozen. They're delicious lightly steamed. The pods can be popped open after cooking, making it easy for diners to remove the beans. (The pods are not eaten.) This delicately flavored dish is good served cold, so it's perfect for parties.

MAKES 4 SERVINGS

1 pound boneless, skinless chicken breasts

2 tablespoons grated fresh ginger

3 tablespoons finely chopped shallots

½ teaspoon ground coriander

2 tablespoons rice vinegar

3 tablespoons fresh orange juice

1 teaspoon dark sesame oil

8 ounces fresh or frozen edamame (green soybeans), in the pod

Salt and freshly ground pepper

Put the chicken in a shallow, nonreactive dish. In a bowl, combine the ginger with the shallots, coriander, vinegar, orange juice, and oil. Pour over the chicken. Refrigerate for 1 to 4 hours.

Fill a wok one-half to two-thirds full of water and bring to a boil over high heat. Reduce the heat to medium and fit an oiled steamer rack or bamboo steamer in the wok. If using a bamboo steamer, set an oiled heatproof plate in it. Remove the chicken from the marinade and arrange it on the rack or plate. Spoon the ginger and shallots from the marinade over the chicken and scatter the edamame around the chicken. Cover and steam for 5 to 7

minutes, or until the chicken is no longer pink on the outside and the edamame are just cooked through. (Remove one of the beans from a pod and bite into it. It should have a firm yet tender texture. If it's hard, it needs more steaming.) Transfer the edamame to a plate. Cover the wok and continue steaming the chicken for 5 to 7 minutes, or until just cooked through in the center.

Transfer the chicken to the plate with the edamame. Season with salt and pepper to taste. Serve warm, or slice the chicken and refrigerate with the edamame to serve cold. To eat the beans, diners simply pop them out of the pods.

STEAMED SALMON WITH WILD RICE BLEND

Fish and wild rice have long been culinary partners, especially in the upper Midwest. We like this dish with a mix of wild, black, and red rices. You can find such blends at natural-foods stores and some supermarkets.

MAKES 4 SERVINGS

Rice

1 cup wild rice blend, rinsed

2 cups water

2 green onions, white part only, minced

2 teaspoons unsalted butter

½ teaspoon salt

3 tablespoons minced fresh dillweed

2 tablespoons fresh or dried dill, or 4 or 5 bay leaves (optional)

Leaf or romaine lettuce leaves for lining steamer

4 center-cut salmon steaks (about 6 ounces each)

Salt and freshly ground pepper

Fresh dill sprigs for garnishing

To make the rice: In a nonstick wok or a saucepan, combine the rice, water, green onions, butter, and salt. Bring to a boil, cover, and reduce the heat to low. Simmer for 40 to 45 minutes, or until the rice is tender. Transfer the rice to a serving platter and keep warm. Just before serving, toss the rice with the dillweed.

Fill the wok one-half to two-thirds full of water, add the fresh or dried dill, if using, and bring to a boil over high heat. Reduce the heat to medium and fit a steamer rack or bamboo steamer in the wok. Line the rack or bottom of the steamer with the lettuce leaves. Set the salmon on the lettuce leaves. Cover and steam for 6 to 8 minutes, or until the fish is slightly firm to the touch and flakes easily when prodded gently with a fork.

Using a spatula, transfer the salmon to individual plates and serve with the rice alongside, or spoon some of the rice in the center of each plate and top with a salmon steak. Season the salmon with salt and pepper to taste and garnish with dill sprigs.

Every year in late January or early to mid-February (the date changes because it's a lunar holiday), Asian households around the world clean house, buy new clothes, and prepare food for the arrival of the New Year. This holiday is like New Year's Eve, Christmas, and everyone's birthday all rolled into one big party. Although we often refer to it as Chinese New Year, the occasion is celebrated with equal intensity in Vietnam, Korea, Singapore, and anywhere in the world with large populations that trace their ancestry to those places. In Chinese homes, fish is usually on the New Year's table because its name is a pun—the word for fish sounds like the word for "surplus," and abundance is the theme of the holiday. Lettuce or other greens, which resemble money, are served, as are oranges or tangerines (they resemble coins).

VIRGINIA'S LUCKY NEW YEAR'S FISH

Virginia always throws a big party for the Asian New Year, and this fish, a slight variation on the Cantonese classic, is always a hit. She generally serves golden trout, a delicious farm-raised fish with shimmery gold scales. You can substitute any red- or gold-skinned fish, such as red snapper.

MAKES 8 TO 10 SERVINGS AS PART OF A LARGE BANQUET / 4 AS AN ENTRÉE

2 unpeeled cloves garlic, lightly crushed

Leaf or romaine lettuce leaves for lining steamer and platter

2 tablespoons black bean–garlic sauce

2 golden trout (about 1 pound each), or 1 red snapper (about 2 pounds)

1 bunch scallions, halved lengthwise, then cut into 2-inch pieces

1 tablespoon peeled, minced fresh ginger

1 tablespoon soy sauce

1 tablespoon dry white wine

Orange slices for garnishing

Green Onion brushes (see page 201) for garnishing (optional)

Fill a wok one-half to two-thirds full of water, add the garlic, and bring to a boil over high heat. Reduce the heat to medium and fit a steamer rack or bamboo steamer in the wok. Line the rack or bottom of the steamer with lettuce leaves.

Dab the black bean sauce over the fish and in the cavity, skipping the heads and tails. Put a few of the scallion pieces and a little of the ginger in each cavity. Arrange the fish on the lettuce leaves in the steamer. You will have to curve the fish and may have to overlap the heads or tails to make them fit. Scatter the remaining scallions and ginger evenly over the fish. Sprinkle with the soy sauce and wine. Cover and steam for 15 to 20 minutes, or until the fish is opaque in the center and flakes easily when prodded gently with a fork. Check the water level halfway through the cooking time and add more boiling water as needed.

Meanwhile, line a serving platter with lettuce leaves. Using 2 spatulas, carefully transfer the fish to the platter. Garnish with orange slices and scallion brushes, if using. Serve immediately.

GARLICKY STEAMED MUSSELS

*Briny-sweet mussels combine beautifully with pungent garlic. Because the liquid is reduced before serving,
be sure to use a lower-salt broth. Otherwise, the juices will be too salty. The mussels are best served in soup bowls,
accompanied by plenty of bread for sopping up the juices.*

MAKES 8 SERVINGS AS AN APPETIZER / 4 AS AN ENTRÉE

2 pounds (45 to 50) black mussels

3½ cups reduced-sodium chicken broth

3 tablespoons finely chopped fresh basil, or 2 tablespoons finely chopped fresh cilantro

1 stalk lemongrass, tender white part only, chopped (optional)

2 tablespoons finely chopped garlic (6 to 8 medium cloves)

Freshly ground pepper

Rinse the mussels under cold running water and snip off any seaweed "beards." Discard any cracked mussels or any that are open and do not close when lightly tapped.

In a wok, combine the chicken broth, basil, lemongrass (if using), garlic, and plenty of pepper. Bring to a boil over high heat. Reduce the heat to medium and fit a steamer rack or bamboo steamer in the wok. If using a bamboo steamer, set a heatproof plate in it.

Arrange the mussels on the rack or plate. Cover and steam for about 5 minutes, or until the mussels open. Discard any that do not open.

Transfer the mussels to a serving dish. Increase the heat under the wok to high and boil the liquid for 2 to 3 minutes to slightly reduce it. Spoon the liquid over the mussels and serve immediately.

STEAMED EGGS WITH GREEN CHILE

Eggs cooked in the steamer are pretty and nicely formed, like poached eggs.
But steaming is usually less trouble, especially if you don't own an egg poacher.

MAKES 2 TO 4 SERVINGS

Sauce

1 tablespoon olive oil

2 cloves garlic, minced

½ cup finely chopped onion

1 fresh jalapeño or serrano chile, seeded and minced

1 pound tomatillos, husked and finely chopped, or green tomatoes, cored and chopped

2 tablespoons finely chopped fresh cilantro

Salt

4 extra-large eggs

Grated Monterey Jack cheese for serving

Warmed corn tortillas for serving

To make the sauce: In a small wok or heavy saucepan over medium-high heat, heat the oil. Add the garlic, onion, and jalapeño and cook, stirring, for 1 to 2 minutes, or until the onion begins to soften. Add the tomatillos, reduce the heat to medium, and cook for 10 to 12 minutes, or until the tomatillos soften and begin to give off liquid. Add a little water if the sauce starts to stick. Stir in the cilantro and salt to taste. The sauce may be covered and refrigerated for up to two days. Reheat just before serving.

Fill a wok one-half to two-thirds full of water and bring to a boil over high heat. Fit a bamboo steamer in the wok and set an oiled heatproof plate in the steamer, or invert a custard cup or other heatproof cup in the wok and set an oiled heatproof plate atop it.

Cover the wok or steamer until the plate gets hot. Gently break the eggs onto the plate, keeping them separate as much as possible. Cover and steam for 3 to 5 minutes, or until the whites and yolks are set.

Using a spatula, transfer the eggs to individual plates. Top with some of the warm green chile sauce (you will have extra) and sprinkle with the cheese. Serve immediately with the tortillas.

SUMMER VEGETABLE SALAD WITH PARMESAN CROUTONS

As spring eases into summer, this warm, brightly flavored salad hits the spot. To infuse the vegetables with herbal flavor, reserve the tarragon or mint stems and add them, along with a few leaves, to the steaming water.

MAKES 6 TO 8 SERVINGS AS A SIDE DISH / 4 AS AN ENTRÉE

Croutons

1 skinny baguette (about 10 ounces)

2 tablespoons extra-virgin olive oil

2 ounces freshly grated Parmesan

Dressing

2 tablespoons rice vinegar

1 teaspoon honey

1 tablespoon finely chopped fresh tarragon or mint

3 tablespoons extra-virgin olive oil

Vegetables

8 baby carrots, halved lengthwise

1 pound asparagus, trimmed and cut into 2-inch lengths

1 cup sugar snap peas or snow peas

1 bunch baby spinach, trimmed and rinsed

Salt and freshly ground pepper

To make the croutons: Preheat the oven to 400°F. Cut the bread into ¼-inch slices. Brush one side of each slice lightly with olive oil, then sprinkle lightly with the cheese. Bake for 8 to 10 minutes, or until golden and crisp. Transfer to a rack to cool. The croutons will keep at room temperature, loosely covered, for 1 to 2 days.

To make the dressing: In a small nonreactive bowl or glass measuring cup, whisk together the vinegar, honey, tarragon, and oil. Set aside. Whisk again just before using.

To steam the vegetables: Fill a wok one-half to two-thirds full of water and bring to a boil over high heat. Reduce the heat to medium and fit an oiled steamer rack or bamboo steamer in the wok. If using a bamboo steamer, set an oiled heatproof plate in it.

Arrange the vegetables on the rack or plate, overlapping them but trying to keep them as close to a single layer as possible. Put the longer-cooking vegetables in the steamer first and add the short-cooking vegetables last. Cover the wok and steam the vegetables in batches for 1 to 8 minutes, depending on the vegetable. The spinach should be just wilted; the other vegetables should be tender-crisp. The baby carrots and asparagus will take 5 to 8 minutes to steam; the peas, 2 to 3 minutes; and the spinach, 1 to 2 minutes.

Transfer the vegetables to a bowl. Add enough dressing to thoroughly moisten them (you may not need all the dressing) and toss to mix. Season with salt and pepper to taste. Arrange the croutons on top of or alongside the vegetables. Serve warm or at room temperature. The salad will keep, covered and refrigerated, for 1 to 2 days. Bring to room temperature before serving.

AUTUMN VEGETABLE SALAD WITH BLUE CHEESE CROUTONS

*The pungency of blue cheese and the evergreen sharpness of thyme pay tribute to the deep-toned
hues and flavors of autumn. To add a hint of herbal flavor to the vegetables, put a few thyme sprigs in the steaming water.*

MAKES 6 TO 8 SERVINGS AS A SIDE DISH / 4 AS AN ENTRÉE

Croutons

1 skinny baguette (about 10 ounces)

2 tablespoons extra-virgin olive oil

3 ounces blue cheese, finely crumbled

Dressing

2 tablespoons red wine vinegar

2 teaspoons firmly packed brown sugar

1 teaspoon soy sauce

2 teaspoons fresh thyme leaves, or ½ teaspoon dried thyme leaves

3 tablespoons extra-virgin olive oil

Vegetables

1 medium sweet potato or yam (about 8 ounces), peeled and cut into ¼-inch slices

1 small eggplant (about 8 ounces), cut into ¼-inch slices

4 baby carrots, halved lengthwise

2 cloves elephant garlic, peeled and halved lengthwise

1 small bunch kale, leaves stripped from stems and stems discarded

Salt and freshly ground pepper

To make the croutons: Preheat the oven to 400°F. Cut the bread into ¼-inch slices. Brush one side of each slice lightly with olive oil, then sprinkle lightly with the cheese. Bake for 8 to 10 minutes, or until golden and crisp. Transfer to a rack to cool. The croutons will keep at room temperature, loosely covered, for 1 to 2 days.

To make the dressing: In a small nonreactive bowl or glass measuring cup, whisk together the vinegar, brown sugar, soy sauce, thyme, and oil. Set aside. Whisk again just before using.

To steam the vegetables: Fill a wok one-half to two-thirds full of water and bring to a boil over high heat. Reduce the heat to medium and fit an oiled steamer rack or bamboo steamer in the wok. If using a bamboo steamer, set an oiled heatproof plate in it.

Arrange the vegetables on the rack or plate, overlapping them but trying to keep them as close to a single layer as possible. Put the longer-cooking vegetables in the steamer first and add the short-cooking vegetables last. Cover the wok and steam the vegetables in batches for 4 to 12 minutes, depending on the vegetable. The kale should be wilted, the eggplant should be soft, and the other vegetables should be tender but not mushy. The sweet potato and eggplant will take 10 to 12 minutes to steam; the carrots and garlic 5 to 8 minutes; and the kale 4 to 5 minutes.

Transfer the vegetables to a bowl. Add enough dressing to thoroughly moisten them (you may not need all the dressing) and toss to mix. Season with salt and pepper to taste. Arrange the croutons on top of or alongside the vegetables. Serve warm or at room temperature. The salad will keep, covered and refrigerated, for 1 to 2 days. Bring to room temperature before serving.

BROCCOFLOWER ON A BED OF LEEKS AND CARROTS

Broccoflower is a cross between broccoli and cauliflower. It has a mild, cauliflower-like flavor and a gorgeous bright-green hue. It is rich in vitamin C and contains iron. To preserve its good looks, the broccoflower is steamed whole in this recipe.

MAKES 4 TO 6 SERVINGS

1 head broccoflower or cauliflower

2 tablespoons unsalted butter

2 large shallots, minced

3 large leeks, white part only, sliced lengthwise, thoroughly cleaned, and cut crosswise into thin slices

1 cup grated carrots

¾ teaspoon dried tarragon

½ cup chicken or vegetable broth, plus more as needed

⅓ cup sliced almonds

Fill a wok one-half to two-thirds full of water and bring to a boil over high heat. Reduce the heat to medium and fit a steamer rack or bamboo steamer in the wok. If using a bamboo steamer, set a heatproof plate in it. Place the broccoflower in the center of the rack or plate. Cover and steam for 20 to 35 minutes, depending on size, or until the broccoflower is tender but not mushy. Check the water level halfway through the cooking time and add more boiling water as needed. Transfer the broccoflower to a serving plate.

Meanwhile, in another wok or in a saucepan over medium heat, melt the butter. Add the shallots, leeks, carrots, and tarragon and cook for 2 minutes. Add the chicken broth and cook, stirring occasionally, for about 10 minutes, or until the leeks are tender. Add more chicken broth if needed.

Spoon the leek mixture into a serving dish and set the hot broccoflower in the center. Sprinkle with the almonds. Serve immediately, using a knife to cut the broccoflower into wedges.

WHITE CHOCOLATE BREAD PUDDING WITH RASPBERRIES

Barbara grew up in a household that embraced not only a loving mother but also a grandmother who was very creative in the kitchen. One of Barbara's early memories is of her grandmother saving leftover pieces of bread each week, then creating a special pudding on Friday. Each bread pudding would be different, depending on the fruit that was available: pears, apples, berries, or dried fruits such as raisins or apricots. Grandma would surely approve of this rich bread pudding made with croissants and raspberries.

MAKES 6 SERVINGS

2 cups milk or half-and-half

4 ounces best-quality white chocolate, cut into small pieces

6 cups packed torn croissants

4 eggs

¾ cup sugar

1 teaspoon vanilla extract

2 tablespoons unsalted butter, melted

¾ teaspoon ground cinnamon

Fresh raspberries for serving

Sweetened whipped cream for serving

It bears a French name, but the croissant was not born in France. According to legend, when the Ottoman Turks lay siege to Vienna in 1683, the city's bakers, who were working day and night to feed the city's starving residents, heard the Turks attempting to tunnel through Vienna's walls in the wee hours of the morning. They alerted the Austrian troops and their allies, and the city was saved. The Empress of Austria commissioned Vienna's bakers to create a crescent-shaped roll, called a kipfel. The design came from the crescent on the Turkish flag. By eating the rolls, the Viennese could symbolically re-create their victory. Marie Antoinette, an Austrian, brought the kipfel to France when she married the prince who would become Louis XVI. The roll was far more popular than the marriage. The French added more yeast and more butter to make a rich, flaky pastry. The rest, as they say, is history.

In a saucepan over medium heat, heat the milk for 3 to 4 minutes, or until very hot. Add the white chocolate, and stir until it is melted and smooth. Set aside to cool.

Put the croissant pieces in a 2-quart heatproof bowl or soufflé dish. Stir in the cooled chocolate mixture and let stand for 10 minutes.

Meanwhile, in another bowl, whisk the eggs and sugar for 1 to 2 minutes, or until light. (Or, in the large bowl of an electric mixer, beat on medium speed for 1 to 2 minutes.) Mix in the vanilla, butter, and cinnamon. Add the egg mixture to the croissant mixture and stir well. Cover the bowl with heavy-duty aluminum foil.

Fill a wok one-half to two-thirds full of water and bring to a boil over high heat. Reduce the heat to medium and fit a steamer rack in the wok, or invert a custard cup or other heatproof cup in the wok and set a heatproof plate atop it.

Set the bowl on the rack or plate. Cover and steam for 1¾ to 2 hours, or until a knife inserted into the center of the pudding comes out clean. Check the water level occasionally and add more boiling water as needed.

Remove the bowl from the wok and let the pudding cool. This is good slightly warm or at room temperature.

To serve, spoon the pudding into dessert bowls, sprinkle with raspberries, and top with a dab of sweetened whipped cream.

CHRISTMAS FIGGY PUDDING

*The English plum pudding, studded with dried fruits and nuts and soaked in spirits,
dates back to at least Victorian times and is a star on the Cratchits' holiday table in Charles Dickens' A Christmas Carol.
Giving the pudding a bath in rum and letting it age improves the flavor.*

MAKES 6 SERVINGS

Pudding

1 cup chopped candied fruit

1½ cups chopped dried figs

⅓ cup ground walnuts

2 cups all-purpose flour

⅓ cup vegetable shortening

¼ cup light unsulphured molasses

¼ cup firmly packed dark brown sugar

3 eggs

¾ teaspoon baking soda

1 teaspoon baking powder

1 teaspoon ground cinnamon

½ teaspoon ground ginger

½ teaspoon salt

¼ teaspoon ground cloves

½ cup milk

¼ cup dark rum, plus ½ cup dark rum if storing pudding

Rum Hard Sauce

¾ cup (1½ sticks) unsalted butter, at room temperature

1½ cups confectioners' sugar

2 tablespoons rum, or to taste

To make the pudding: Butter a 1½-quart pudding mold, soufflé dish, or other bowl suitable for steaming.

Put the candied fruit, figs, and walnuts in a small bowl and toss with ¼ cup of the flour. Set aside.

In the large bowl of an electric mixer, beat the shortening with the molasses and brown sugar on medium speed until light. Beat in the eggs, one at a time. In another bowl, stir together the remaining 1¾ cups flour, the baking soda, baking powder, cinnamon, ginger, salt, and cloves, then stir into the batter. Mix in the milk, the reserved fruits and nuts, and the ¼ cup rum. Spoon the batter into the prepared mold and cover with buttered heavy-duty aluminum foil.

Fill a wok one-half to two-thirds full of water and bring to a boil over high heat. Reduce the heat to medium and fit a steamer rack in the wok, or invert a custard cup or other heatproof cup in the wok and set a heatproof plate atop it. Place the pudding mold on the rack or plate. Cover and steam for 1½ to 2 hours, or until a knife inserted into the center of the pudding comes out clean. Check the water level occasionally and add more boiling water as needed.

Remove the mold from the wok and let the pudding cool. To unmold, run a knife between the pudding and the mold and invert onto a serving dish. Serve slightly warm or at room temperature.

To store the pudding, cut a piece of cheesecloth large enough to cover the pudding. Soak the cloth in the ½ cup rum. Wrap the pudding in the cloth and store in an airtight tin or wrap in heavy-duty aluminum foil. The pudding can last a few weeks, but sprinkle a few tablespoons of rum over the top now and then to keep it from drying out.

To make the rum hard sauce: Prepare the sauce while the pudding is steaming or the day you plan to serve it. Using an electric mixer, a food processor fitted with the steel blade, or a bowl and wooden spoon, beat together the butter and confectioner's sugar until light. Pour in the rum and mix or process until combined.

Spoon the sauce into a small bowl and serve at room temperature.

CHOCOLATE CUSTARDS WITH COFFEE SYRUP

Instead of custard cups, you can use coffee cups or teacups (not mugs). If you're avoiding caffeine, use decaffeinated coffee in the syrup. Or, for a quicker and even more adult dessert, skip the syrup and drizzle coffee liqueur over the custards just before serving.

MAKES 6 SERVINGS

Custards

2 cups milk

4 ounces bittersweet or semisweet chocolate, chopped

1 egg

2 egg yolks

1 teaspoon vanilla extract

1 teaspoon cornstarch

½ teaspoon ground cinnamon

⅛ teaspoon salt

Coffee Syrup

½ cup firmly packed light brown sugar

⅓ cup brewed espresso (or extra-strong regular coffee), hot or cold

½ teaspoon vanilla extract

To make the custards: In a saucepan over medium heat, heat 1 cup of the milk for 3 to 4 minutes, or until very hot. Add the chocolate, and stir until the chocolate is melted and smooth. Whisk in the remaining 1 cup milk, then whisk in the egg and egg yolks, vanilla, cornstarch, cinnamon, and salt until smooth.

Butter six 6-ounce heatproof custard cups. Pour or ladle the custard mixture into the cups, filling them about two-thirds full.

Fill a wok one-half to two-thirds full of water and bring to a boil over high heat. Reduce the heat to medium and fit a steamer rack or bamboo steamer in the wok. If using a bamboo steamer, set a heatproof plate in it. Arrange the custard cups in a circle on the rack or plate and cover with a sheet of heavy-duty aluminum foil. Cover and steam for 30 to 35 minutes, or until a knife inserted into the center of a custard comes out clean. Check the water level halfway through the cooking time and add more boiling water as needed.

To make the coffee syrup: While the custards steam, in a small saucepan over high heat, combine the brown sugar, espresso, and vanilla. Heat for about 2 minutes, or until the brown sugar has dissolved and the mixture is syrupy. Set aside to cool.

Transfer the custards to a wire rack and cool for 15 to 20 minutes, then refrigerate for at least 2 hours. Just before serving, unmold the custards, if desired, by running a knife between each custard and the cup; then inverting the cup onto a dessert plate and tapping to release the custard onto the plate. Or, serve the custards in their cups. (This is best if you are using coffee cups.) Spoon some of the coffee syrup over each custard.

STEAMED CHOCOLATE CAKE

Many thanks to Barbara's friend Eva for giving us this recipe from her mother, Margaret Fishell. Margaret, who inherited the recipe from her mother-in-law, brought it with her when she fled Czechoslovakia just before World War II. The cake was a treat that Grandmother Fishell served on special occasions.

MAKES 6 TO 8 SERVINGS

6 eggs, separated

½ cup (1 stick) unsalted butter at room temperature, cut into pieces

⅓ cup sugar

1¼ cups (5 ounces) finely ground almonds

8 ounces German (sweet) chocolate, melted

Sweetened whipped cream for serving

Butter an 8-cup fluted or regular tube pan that does not have a removable bottom.

In the large bowl of an electric mixer, beat the egg whites on high speed until stiff and glossy but not dry. Set aside.

In another mixer bowl, beat the butter and sugar on medium speed until light. Mix in the egg yolks. Add the almonds and stir to combine. Blend in the chocolate. Using a rubber spatula, gently stir in the egg whites. Spoon the batter into the prepared pan and cover with a tight-fitting lid or heavy-duty aluminum foil.

Fill a wok one-half to two-thirds full of water and bring to a boil over high heat. Reduce the heat to medium and fit a steamer rack in the wok, or invert a custard cup or other heatproof cup in the wok and set a heatproof plate atop it. Place the cake pan on the rack or plate. Cover and steam for 1 hour, or until a knife inserted into the center of the cake comes out clean. Check the water level occasionally and add more boiling water as needed.

Preheat the oven to 350°F. Using pot holders, remove the pan from the wok. Uncover slightly and put in the oven for 5 minutes, to help dry out any excess liquid in the cake. Cool for 5 minutes, then invert the cake onto a serving plate. Serve warm with sweetened whipped cream.

CHAPTER SIX

ALL WET

BRAISING AND SIMMERING

IF STEAMING IS A SAUNA, BRAISING IS A RELAXING BATH. 🥣 ALTHOUGH STIR-FRYING GETS THE MOST ATTENTION, WOKS TRADITIONALLY HAVE BEEN USED FOR NEARLY EVERY TYPE OF COOKING TECHNIQUE, INCLUDING BRAISING, A METHOD THAT MAKES TOUGHER, LESS EXPENSIVE CUTS OF MEAT MORE PALATABLE AND BLENDS FLAVORS INTO A HARMONIOUS MEDLEY. BRAISING IS MUCH MORE COMMON IN CHINA THAN YOU WOULD GUESS FROM CHINESE RESTAURANT MENUS IN WESTERN COUNTRIES, WHICH EMPHASIZE STIR-FRIED AND DEEP-FRIED DISHES.

Like steaming, braising relies on moist heat, except that the foods are cooked in, rather than over, liquid. They also are usually cooked for a longer time. While steaming enhances the individual flavors of foods, braising melds them into a delicious whole. It helps to tenderize and flavor poultry, beef, fish, and vegetables, and to blend various spices. Unlike steaming or stir-frying, braising works well with very lean cuts of meat. Beef stew and chili are classic examples of Western-style braised dishes.

Braising often is combined with other cooking techniques. For example, you may stir-fry or brown meat first to seal in its juices, then add liquid and braise it. While many braised dishes (such as chili) cook slowly over medium to low heat, braising is not always slow cooking. What makes a dish braised, in our opinion, is the fact that the liquid is used not only to cook the food, but also to flavor it. Braised dishes also are cooked in a covered pan.

Because braising often involves long cooking times and requires small amounts of liquid, making it more likely that foods will stick to the pan, we recommend using a wok with a nonstick coating.

Braised foods often contain several different spices or seasonings. Because the idea is to blend flavors, dishes such as curries, stews, and chilis often taste better a day or two after they're cooked, making them ideal for parties when you want to cook in advance. Refrigerate the food and reheat just before serving.

Simmering requires more liquid and less cooking time than braising. It is a way to gently cook foods when you want to retain their shape, when you want to heat them just long enough so they absorb the flavors of the cooking liquid, or when boiling would toughen them or drive off the flavor (or, in the case of rice, make them stick). It's very similar to steaming except that the food is cooked in, rather than over, the liquid.

There is only one rule for braised and simmered foods: Take it easy. Keep the liquid at or below a gentle simmer. Boiling toughens meats and can reduce the amount of liquid too quickly, causing foods to scorch. Braising is also a hands-off method. Other than an occasional stir or peek to make sure the liquid is not evaporating too quickly, leave braised foods alone to gently bubble into tenderness.

You need no special equipment to braise or simmer—just a wok, preferably with a nonstick coating, and a wooden spoon. For starchy foods such as risotto, an electric wok, with its precise heat controls, comes in handy.

CURRIED BEEF WITH BASMATI PILAF

This dish is inspired by the curries popular throughout much of Asia but is greatly streamlined for harried Western cooks.

MAKES 4 SERVINGS

2 tablespoons vegetable oil

1 pound beef sirloin, trimmed and cut into ½-inch strips

1 medium onion, thinly sliced

1 tablespoon grated fresh ginger

3 tablespoons curry powder

½ cup beef broth, plus more as needed

2 teaspoons flour

1 cup plain yogurt

½ cup drained, canned chickpeas

1 packed cup trimmed and washed spinach leaves

Basmati Pilaf (page 162), or plain cooked basmati rice for serving

In a nonstick wok over medium-high heat, heat the oil. Add the beef and cook, turning once or twice, for 3 to 4 minutes, or until browned on all sides. Using a slotted spoon, transfer the beef to a plate and set aside.

Add the onion and ginger to the wok, reduce the heat to medium, and cook for 4 to 5 minutes, or until tender. Return the beef to the wok. Stir in the curry powder and cook for about 1 minute, or until the ingredients are combined. In a small dish, whisk together the beef broth, flour, and yogurt. Add to the wok and stir well. Cover and cook for about 1 hour, or until the beef is tender and the sauce is thick. Check occasionally and add more broth as needed. Stir in the chickpeas and spinach and cook for 2 to 3 minutes, or until hot.

Serve the curry over the pilaf.

CONTINUED →

BASMATI PILAF

With its nutty, house-filling fragrance and dry, almost lacy texture, basmati is a justifiably famous member of the rice family. It hails from northern India, but basmati-style rices are now grown elsewhere, including Texas.

MAKES 4 TO 6 SERVINGS

1 tablespoon unsalted butter

4 green onions, white part only, finely chopped

1 cup basmati rice

1 cup grated carrots

½ cup frozen or fresh peas

2¼ cups chicken broth

Salt and freshly ground white pepper

In a nonstick wok over medium heat, melt the butter. Add the green onions and cook for 4 to 5 minutes, or until tender. Add the rice and sauté for 2 to 3 minutes. Stir in the carrots, peas, and chicken broth. Bring to a boil, reduce the heat to low, cover, and simmer for 20 minutes, or until the rice is tender.

Season with salt and white pepper to taste.

LAMB STEW WITH PINE NUTS

*The rich, almost gamy flavor of lamb and the sweetly resinous essence of pine nuts are a great match.
Still a thrifty New Englander at heart, Barbara created this stew when she had some lamb left over after making kabobs.
It turned out very well indeed.*

MAKES 4 SERVINGS

2 tablespoons vegetable oil or olive oil

1¼ to 1½ pounds boneless lamb shoulder, cut into 1-inch cubes

1 cup chicken broth, plus more as needed

4 cloves garlic, minced

1 large onion, thinly sliced

3 large boiling potatoes, peeled and cut into ¼-inch slices

4 large carrots, cut into ¼-inch slices

3 large oil-packed dried tomatoes, drained and chopped

½ teaspoon dried oregano

Salt and freshly ground pepper

¼ cup pine nuts, preferably toasted (see page 209)

In a wok, preferably nonstick, over medium-high heat, heat the oil. Add the lamb and cook, turning, for 4 to 5 minutes, or until browned on all sides. Add the 1 cup chicken broth, the garlic, onion, potatoes, carrots, dried tomatoes, and oregano. Reduce the heat to medium-low, cover, and cook for 1½ hours, or until the meat is tender.

Stir occasionally, adding more broth as needed to keep the stew from sticking. A small amount of liquid will form in the bottom of the wok; stir to incorporate it into the stew. Season with salt and pepper to taste.

Spoon the stew into individual bowls and sprinkle with the pine nuts. Serve hot.

In Italy, pine nuts are called pignolia, *while in the U.S. Southwest, they're known as* piñon. *The nuts are harvested from pine trees in both those places as well as in China, Mexico, and northern Africa. Wherever they come from, they're delicious. Traditional cultures relied on pine nuts for the concentrated energy they provide: 2 tablespoons of the nuts supply more than 400 calories and nearly 9 grams of fat. Modern cultures use them more sparingly, prizing these nuts for their rich yet resinous flavor. Pine nuts go rancid quickly, so store them in the refrigerator or freezer. They taste best toasted (see page 209).*

BURMESE SPAGHETTI

Despite the name, this rich curry is about as American as it gets. It is inspired by a coconut-based curry that's the national dish of Myanmar (Burma), but it was taught to Virginia by a Pakistani friend who learned how to make it from his mother. Like many immigrants, he adapted the original to his culture (the fried onions are a Pakistani/Indian touch), his tastes, and readily available supermarket ingredients. We've adapted it even further. The gravy is very rich, and a little goes a long way. The accompaniments are crucial to this dish, but can be prepared ahead of time.

MAKES 6 TO 8 SERVINGS

2 medium onions, coarsely chopped

4 or 5 cloves garlic, coarsely chopped

1½-inch piece fresh ginger, peeled and coarsely chopped

½ to 1 teaspoon cayenne pepper

1 teaspoon turmeric

2 cups coconut milk

2 teaspoons dark sesame oil

1 tablespoon peanut oil

1 pound ground lean beef

¾ cup water, plus more as needed

1 teaspoon dried shrimp paste, or 1 tablespoon fish sauce

Salt

1 pound spaghetti

Accompaniments (choose at least 2)

Chopped green onions

Chopped fresh cilantro

Deep-fried onions and garlic (page 201)

Lemon wedges

Ground or crushed red chiles

In a blender or food processor, combine about half the onions with the garlic, ginger, cayenne pepper to taste, turmeric, and coconut milk. Process until the solid ingredients are finely minced. Set aside.

In a wok, preferably nonstick, over medium-high heat, heat the sesame and peanut oils. Add the remaining chopped onions and stir-fry for 6 to 7 minutes, or until browned and tender. Add the ground beef and cook for 4 to 5 minutes, or just until no longer pink.

Add the coconut milk mixture, the ¾ cup water, and shrimp paste. Bring to a simmer, reduce the heat to medium-low, cover, and cook for 1½ to 2 hours, or until the liquid has turned into a thick, somewhat oily gravy and the spice flavors have blended. Check occasionally and add more water as needed. Season with salt to taste. Serve immediately, or cool, cover, and refrigerate for up to 2 days.

Fill a large wok, preferably nonstick, about half full of salted water and bring to boil over high heat. Add the pasta and cook according to the package directions. Drain. Mound the pasta on plates and spoon the curry over it. Serve with your choice of accompaniments.

HOT POT

This beautiful meal is cooked at the table by the guests themselves, making it the ideal interactive centerpiece for a party. It requires an electric wok. You can use canned chicken broth, but homemade stock will taste much better.

MAKES 6 SERVINGS

8 cups chicken stock

½ pound boneless, skinless chicken breasts, cut into bite-sized pieces

3 cups sliced romaine lettuce

1 pound raw large shrimp, peeled, deveined, and butterflied (see page 207)

8 ounces baby spinach, washed and drained

12 ounces firm tofu, cut into ½-inch cubes

6 green onions, white part only, minced

1 can (6½ ounces) sliced water chestnuts, drained

2 red or green bell peppers, seeded, deribbed, and sliced

Hoisin sauce for serving

Soy sauce for serving

Chile sauce for serving

Cooked rice or noodles for serving

The first time we ordered a hot pot in Hong Kong, we quickly learned what freshness really means to the Chinese. The shrimp were still waving their antennae as they were marched to the table to meet their doom. Because the average American is more squeamish, we recommend serving more docile, if not quite as fresh, shrimp.

In an electric wok set on high heat, heat the chicken stock. Meanwhile, arrange the food decoratively on plates and set around the wok. For example, place the chicken slices on a plate with some of the lettuce, and the shrimp on two or three plates with the spinach and maybe some green onions on top. Set the hoisin, soy, and chile sauces in small dishes on the table. Encourage diners to add food to the chicken stock. Cover the wok and cook the food on high for about 10 minutes, or until the chicken is cooked through.

Ask diners to transfer the cooked food, using chopsticks and small strainers, into soup bowls. Serve with rice or noodles and pass the sauces at the table. Continue until all of the food has been cooked.

For the final course, ladle the flavorful stock into soup bowls and serve.

CINCINNATI-STYLE TURKEY CHILI

*In Cincinnati, Ohio, chili is more than a dish, it's an obsession. Five-way chili, for diehards, gets its name
from the five layers that make up the dish: spaghetti, meat chili, beans, raw onions, and finely grated Cheddar cheese.
We make it leaner with ground turkey, but you can always use the more traditional ground beef.
Like all chilis, this one tastes even better the next day.*

MAKES 4 TO 6 SERVINGS

2 tablespoons vegetable oil

1¼ pounds ground lean turkey

1 clove garlic, minced

1 small white or yellow onion, chopped

1 can (15 ounces) chopped tomatoes, with juices

½ teaspoon ground cinnamon

½ teaspoon ground allspice

1½ tablespoons chili powder

2 teaspoons ground cumin

1 tablespoon rice wine vinegar

2 large bay leaves

Salt and freshly ground pepper

12 ounces thin spaghetti, cooked according to package directions and drained

1 can (15 ounces) kidney beans, drained and warmed

1 medium red onion, chopped, for garnishing

6 ounces grated Cheddar cheese for garnishing

In a nonstick wok over medium-high heat, heat the oil. Add the turkey, garlic, and white onion. Reduce the heat to medium and cook, stirring occasionally, for 7 to 8 minutes, or until the turkey is cooked through. Add the tomatoes, cinnamon, allspice, chili powder, cumin, vinegar, bay leaves, and salt and pepper to taste. Cover and cook for about 10 minutes, or until bubbling hot. Remove the bay leaves before serving.

To serve, divide the spaghetti among individual plates. (If the spaghetti was cooked ahead of time, place it in a colander and run hot water over it.) Spoon the chili over the spaghetti. Top with the beans and garnish with the red onion and cheese. Serve hot.

Note: Always remove and discard bay leaves before serving a dish. The sharp-edged leaves can be uncomfortable, even dangerous, if they get caught in someone's throat.

CHICKEN-OLIVE TAGINE WITH WHOLE-WHEAT COUSCOUS

A tagine is a Moroccan stew of meat, vegetables, and sometimes fruit, seasoned with a fragrant medley of spices and served over couscous. This quicker-cooking version tastes great on whole-wheat couscous, but regular couscous is fine, or you can substitute noodles or rice. There is plenty of delicious broth, so ladle the tagine into soup bowls and accompany with crusty bread for soaking up the juices.

MAKES 6 SERVINGS

Marinade

1 cup fresh lemon juice

3 cloves garlic, minced

1½ tablespoons fresh thyme leaves, or 1½ teaspoons dried

3 pounds chicken pieces, skinned

2 tablespoons extra-virgin olive oil

1 cup grated carrots

¾ cup chopped fresh flat-leaf parsley

2 cups water or chicken broth

½ teaspoon turmeric

Salt

Cayenne pepper

1 large onion, thinly sliced

⅓ cup kalamata olives

1½ cups whole-wheat couscous, cooked according to package directions

To make the marinade: In a nonreactive bowl, combine the lemon juice, garlic, and thyme.

Pour the marinade into 1 large self-sealing plastic bag or 2 smaller bags. Add the chicken, seal the bag securely, and turn it over so all sides of the chicken are in contact with the marinade. Set the bag in a bowl and refrigerate for 1½ to 2 hours. Drain, reserving the marinade.

In a wok, preferably nonstick, over medium-high to high heat, heat the oil. Add the chicken and cook, turning as needed, for about 8 minutes, or until browned. Stir in the reserved marinade, the carrots, parsley, water, turmeric, and salt and cayenne pepper to taste. Add the onion. Reduce the heat to low, cover, and cook for 15 to 20 minutes, or until the chicken is tender. Stir in the olives.

Serve in soup bowls over a mound of couscous.

MAHOGANY CHICKEN WITH DRIED CRANBERRIES

The soy sauce gives this chicken a deep russet hue, like mahogany. "Red cooking," or simmering foods in a soy-based sauce, is a technique that is popular throughout China. The cranberries, of course, are an American touch. This dish is good with noodles.

MAKES 4 TO 6 SERVINGS

Sauce

2½ cups soy sauce

1½ cups water

2 tablespoons honey

½ teaspoon Chinese five-spice powder

2 lumps rock sugar (see page 214), or 2 tablespoons firmly packed light brown sugar

3 tablespoons oyster sauce

½ teaspoon dark sesame oil

2 whole boneless, skinless chicken breasts (about 1 pound)

¼ cup dried cranberries for garnishing

2 tablespoons chopped fresh chives for garnishing

To make the sauce: In a wok over medium-high heat, combine the soy sauce, water, honey, five-spice powder, sugar, oyster sauce, and sesame oil. Cover and simmer for 5 minutes.

Add the chicken, turning it and spooning the sauce over it so all of the chicken is in contact with the sauce. Reduce the heat to low, cover, and cook for 10 to 12 minutes. Turn off the heat and let the chicken stand in the sauce for 20 minutes.

Remove a piece of chicken and cut into it to make sure there are no traces of pink in the center. If it is not cooked through, return it to the wok and simmer until done. Transfer the chicken to a cutting board and cut into slices. Arrange the slices on a serving plate and garnish with the dried cranberries and chives. Drizzle with a few tablespoons of the sauce. Serve immediately.

WHITEFISH BOIL IN THE STYLE OF DOOR COUNTY

This is a stovetop adaptation of the outdoor fish boil, a long-standing summer tradition with visitors to Door County, Wisconsin. Serve with coleslaw and cherry pie or cobbler.

MAKES 6 SERVINGS

6 ears of corn, silks and husks removed

12 small red potatoes, scrubbed

12 small onions, peeled

2 pounds whitefish fillets, cut into 6 pieces

Lemon or lime wedges for garnishing

Chopped fresh parsley for garnishing

Melted butter for serving

Using a large, heavy knife, cut each ear of corn into 3 pieces. Set aside.

Fill a wok half full of salted water and bring to a boil over high heat. Reduce the heat to medium-high. Add the potatoes and onions and cook for about 15 minutes, or until tender. Reduce the heat to medium. Add the corn and fish. Cook for 6 to 7 minutes, or until the fish is opaque and flakes easily when prodded gently with a fork. Do not overcook the fish.

Using a slotted spoon, gently transfer the fish to a platter and surround it with the potatoes, onions, and corn. Garnish with lemon wedges and parsley, and serve with plenty of melted butter.

The fish boil is a popular tourist draw in Door County, a scenic Wisconsin peninsula that juts into the chilly waters of Lake Michigan. It is prepared outdoors with great pomp. Freshly caught Great Lakes whitefish is cooked in a large drum filled with water set over a wood fire. Just before the cooking ends, more fuel is tossed onto the fire, making the flames leap high and the kettle overflow with a dramatic "whoosh." Supposedly this overboil helps drains off unpleasant fishy-tasting oils, but the oohs and aahs it elicits from the dining tourists are no doubt just as important. The fish is boiled along with potatoes, onions, and sometimes fresh ears of corn. All are served with rivers of melted butter, freshly made coleslaw, and local breads. Dessert is pie made with another Door County specialty, delightfully tart Montmorency cherries.

SALMON AND SQUASH IN RED CURRY

This is a classic example of fusion cooking: squash and salmon, two quintessential North American ingredients, simmered in a Thai curry. The squash, beans, and salmon can be cooked early in the day. Red curry paste, a blend of chiles and herbs, is found in gourmet stores and Asian food stores. Serve this dish with white or black rice.

MAKES 4 SERVINGS

1 medium butternut squash, or 1 large acorn squash (2 to 2½ pounds)

2 cups green beans

2 tablespoons vegetable oil

1 tablespoon unsalted butter

4 salmon fillets (about ¼ pound each)

1 large onion, thinly sliced

2 cloves garlic, minced

1 tablespoon minced fresh lemongrass, tender white part only

1 tablespoon peeled, minced fresh ginger

1 tablespoon red curry paste, or to taste

1¾ cups coconut milk

2 tablespoons fresh lime juice

Halve the squash and remove the seeds. Fill a wok one-half to two-thirds full of water and bring to a boil over high heat. Reduce the heat to medium and fit a steamer rack or a bamboo steamer in the wok. If using a bamboo steamer, set a heatproof plate in it. Place the squash, cut-side down, on the rack or plate, cover, and steam for 8 minutes. Arrange the beans around the squash and steam for 7 to 12 minutes more, or until the beans are tender-crisp and the squash can be easily pierced with a knife. Transfer the squash and beans to plates. When the squash is cool enough to handle, peel it and cut into cubes; you should have about 2 cups.

In a nonstick wok over medium-high heat, heat 1 tablespoon of the oil and melt the butter. Add the salmon, 2 pieces at a time, and cook, turning once, for 5 to 8 minutes, or until it is slightly firm and flakes easily when prodded gently with a fork. Transfer the salmon to a plate. Skin it and cut into chunks. Set aside.

In the wok over medium-high heat, heat the remaining 1 tablespoon oil. Add the onion, garlic, lemongrass, and ginger and stir-fry for a few seconds, or until fragrant. Stir in the red curry paste, coconut milk, lime juice, squash, and beans. Add the salmon. Simmer, stirring occasionally, for 8 to 10 minutes, or until heated through. Serve immediately.

SHRIMP IN GREEN CURRY

Feel free to substitute chunks of firm fish, such as halibut, swordfish, or catfish, for the shrimp in this Thai-inspired dish. You can also add 1 cup drained baby corn or cooked snow peas and 2 or 3 tablespoons Southeast Asian fish sauce. Accompany with white or black rice.

MAKES 4 SERVINGS

2 tablespoons peanut oil

1 pound raw extra-large shrimp, peeled and deveined

4 green onions, white part only, chopped

3 cloves garlic, minced

1 tablespoon peeled, minced fresh ginger

1 tablespoon minced fresh lemongrass, tender white part only

2 tablespoons green curry paste, or to taste

1¾ cups coconut milk

1 tablespoon firmly packed dark brown sugar

¼ cup chicken broth

1½ cups fresh bean sprouts

Chopped fresh cilantro for garnishing (optional)

One image that lingers with us from our Asian travels, especially in Thailand, is that of women grinding spices. Armies of them, it seemed, would sit barefoot, mortars tucked under one arm while they used the pestle in the other hand to pound chiles, garlic, ginger, and spices into fragrant pastes. The bright colors of their clothing and the pungent smells of the seasonings blend into a heady remembrance of the searing heat and brilliant hues of southern Asia. Blenders and food processors are much more convenient (and a long-awaited blessing for so many cooks in Asia). But somehow they're just not the same.

In a wok over medium-high heat, heat the oil. Add the shrimp, green onions, garlic, ginger, and lemongrass. Cook, turning the shrimp as needed, for about 2 minutes, or until they are just cooked through and the seasonings are fragrant. Transfer to a plate and set aside.

In the wok, combine the green curry paste and coconut milk. Simmer for 3 to 4 minutes. Add the brown sugar, broth, and bean sprouts. Return the shrimp mixture to the wok and simmer just until heated through.

Spoon the curry into a serving bowl or into individual soup bowls, sprinkle with chopped cilantro, if using, and serve immediately.

QUICK FEIJOADA WITH GREENS

Feijoada, the famous Brazilian dish of meats served with black bean stew, can be an elaborate preparation, featuring beans cooked from scratch, a huge platter of various fresh and smoked meats, and several accompaniments. This version is much quicker yet still tastes delicious. The greens are optional, but their slight bitterness makes an intriguing counterpoint to the rich beans and meat.

MAKES 4 TO 6 SERVINGS

Greens (optional)

2 medium bunches collard greens (about 1½ pounds total)

1 bacon slice, diced

2 cloves garlic, minced

½ cup water

Salt and freshly ground pepper

Beans and Meat

1 tablespoon olive oil

2 bacon slices, diced

1 pound spicy sausage, such as hot Italian sausage, chorizo, or linguiça, cut into 1½-inch pieces

1 large onion, chopped

5 or 6 cloves garlic, minced

1 to 3 teaspoons hot red pepper sauce

1 cup water

2 cans (15 ounces each) black beans, with liquid

Cooked white rice for serving

Salt and freshly ground pepper

Orange slices for garnishing

Hot red pepper sauce for serving

Legumes and rice are a time-honored combination in many cultures. In the Americas, there's Brazilian feijoada, Cuban black beans and rice, and the New Orleans variation, red beans and rice. All trace their roots to Africa. The pairing of beans (or dried peas) and rice makes an inexpensive, tasty, and filling meal that is rich in protein and other nutrients.

To prepare the greens: Rinse the collard greens and remove the stems. Cut the leaves crosswise into narrow strips.

Heat a small wok or a 2- to 3-quart heavy saucepan over medium-high heat. Add the bacon and fry for about 1 minute, or until almost cooked through. Add the garlic and fry for about 30 seconds, or until fragrant and beginning to turn golden. Add the greens and the water. Reduce the heat to low, cover, and cook for 8 to 10 minutes, or until the greens are thoroughly wilted and tender. Remove from the wok and season with salt and plenty of pepper to taste. Set aside. Reheat just before serving.

To prepare the meat and beans: Preheat the oven to 200°F. In a wok, preferably nonstick, over medium-high heat, heat the oil. Add the bacon and stir-fry for 1 to 2 minutes, or until cooked through but not crisp. Add the sausage and cook, turning, for 3 to 4 minutes, or until browned on all sides. Add the onion and garlic and

stir-fry for 2 to 3 minutes, or until the onion is tender. Stir in hot red pepper sauce to taste and the water. Reduce the heat to medium-low, cover, and cook for 7 to 10 minutes, or until the sausage is just cooked through. Using tongs, transfer the sausage to a heatproof plate and keep warm in the oven.

Add the beans with their liquid to the wok. Increase the heat to medium-high and bring the beans to a simmer. Reduce the heat to medium-low, cover, and simmer for 5 minutes. The beans should be fairly soupy; if they begin to stick to the pan, add a little water.

To serve, spoon the rice into individual soup bowls or plates. Spoon the beans over the rice and top with the sausage. Salt and pepper to taste and garnish each serving with a spoonful of greens and 1 or 2 orange slices. Serve immediately and pass the hot red pepper sauce at the table.

WHITE ASPARAGUS WITH BLACK RICE AND PICKLED GINGER

White asparagus is becoming more widely available in large supermarkets and specialty food stores. If you have difficulty finding it, substitute green asparagus. Garnish this simple yet elegant dish with very thinly sliced, pale Japanese-style pickled ginger, the kind served with sushi.

MAKES 4 SERVINGS

1½ cups black sticky rice, rinsed

1 pound white asparagus

3 tablespoons unsalted butter, melted

Salt and freshly ground pepper

⅓ cup rice vinegar

Pickled ginger for garnishing

Put the rice in a bowl and add enough water to cover by 2 inches. Let stand for at least 5 hours or up to 12 hours. Drain.

Trim the asparagus and peel the bottoms of the stalks if they are woody. Fill a nonstick wok one-half to two-thirds full of water and bring to a boil over high heat. Reduce the heat to medium. Add the asparagus, cover, and simmer for 2 to 3 minutes, or until the asparagus is tender-crisp. Drain and transfer to a plate. Drizzle with the butter and season lightly with salt and pepper to taste.

Discard the asparagus cooking water. Put the rice in the wok and add enough water to cover by 2 inches. Bring to a boil over high heat. Reduce the heat to medium, cover, and cook, stirring occa-sionally and adding more hot water if needed, for 30 to 40 minutes, or until the rice is tender but still slightly chewy. The cooking time depends on how you like the texture of the rice; if you prefer softer rice, let it cook longer. Drain and let cool.

Transfer the rice to a bowl. Add the vinegar and salt and pepper to taste, and toss to mix.

Mound the rice in the center of a serving plate. Arrange the aspara-gus and the pickled ginger decoratively alongside or on top of the rice. Serve warm or at room temperature. You can make the salad up to 1 day in advance, cover and refrigerate, and let it stand at room temperature for 30 minutes before serving.

BLACK RICE SALAD

We're smitten with the gorgeous deep purplish-black hue of black sticky rice. We're just as in love with its nutty flavor. Black sticky rice is available at some markets that carry Thai ingredients (see Sources of Equipment and Ingredients, page 216). You can also make this salad with regular white sticky (glutinous) rice.

MAKES 4 SERVINGS

1½ cups black sticky rice, rinsed

1½ cups shredded red cabbage

1 cup shredded carrots

1 small red onion, thinly sliced

Vinaigrette

1 teaspoon stone-ground mustard

⅓ cup extra-virgin olive oil

3 tablespoons balsamic vinegar

Salt and freshly ground pepper

Put the rice in a bowl and add enough water to cover by 2 inches. Let stand for at least 5 hours or up to 12 hours. Drain.

Put the rice in a nonstick wok and add enough water to cover by 2 inches. Bring to a boil over high heat. Reduce the heat to medium, cover, and cook, stirring occasionally and adding more hot water if needed, for 30 to 40 minutes, or until the rice is tender but still slightly chewy. The cooking time depends on how you like the texture of the rice; if you prefer softer rice, let it cook longer. Drain and let cool.

Transfer the rice to a bowl. Add the cabbage, carrots, and red onion and toss to mix.

To make the vinaigrette: In a small bowl, whisk together the mustard, oil, vinegar, and salt and pepper to taste. Add to the rice mixture and toss well. Taste and adjust the seasonings if needed.

Serve the salad at room temperature. You can make the salad up to 1 day in advance, cover, and refrigerate, then let it stand at room temperature for 30 minutes before serving.

SAFFRON RISOTTO WITH GOAT CHEESE

The tang of the goat cheese complements the mild flavor of the rice. Any leftover risotto can be used to make pancakes. This is one of the few cases where we recommend using an electric wok. Its lower, steady heat is perfect for slow-simmered dishes such as risotto. If you don't have an electric wok, use one with a nonstick coating.

MAKES 4 TO 6 SERVINGS

½ teaspoon saffron threads

4 cups vegetable or chicken stock or broth, or as needed

4 tablespoons unsalted butter

2 large shallots, chopped

1½ cups Arborio or other Italian superfino rice

¾ cup dry white wine

½ cup (2 ounces) crumbled plain goat cheese

1 to 2 tablespoons finely chopped fresh basil

Salt and freshly ground pepper

In a medium saucepan, bring the stock to a boil, then remove from the heat. Stir the saffron into the hot stock. Keep warm over low heat.

In an electric wok set on medium heat, melt 2 tablespoons of the butter. Add the shallots and cook, stirring with a wooden spoon, for about 5 minutes, or until tender. Add the rice and stir-fry for 1 minute to coat with the butter. Stir in the wine and cook for 2 to 3 minutes, or until absorbed. Add the stock, ½ to ¾ cup at a time,

cooking and stirring for 5 to 6 minutes, or until each batch of stock is absorbed. Continue in this manner, scraping down the rice from the sides of the wok, for 25 to 35 minutes, or until the rice is creamy and tender but not mushy.

Stir in the goat cheese, basil, and salt and pepper to taste. Add the remaining 2 tablespoons butter and stir until melted. Spoon the risotto onto plates or into a serving bowl. Serve immediately.

CAJUN RATATOUILLE OVER GREENS

Although the ingredients are Mediterranean, and the seasonings Cajun, this recipe draws on the most sacred of Asian food concepts: the interplay of sweet and sour, hot and cold, crisp and soft.

MAKES 6 SERVINGS

4 tablespoons extra-virgin olive oil

3 cloves garlic, minced

1 large onion, thinly sliced

1 large eggplant, peeled and cut into ½- to ¾-inch dice

1 medium zucchini, cut into ¼-inch slices

2 red or green bell peppers, seeded, deribbed, and coarsely chopped

3 cups chopped fresh tomatoes, or 1 can (28 ounces) chopped tomatoes, with juices

½ cup tomato juice, or as needed (if using fresh tomatoes)

¼ cup red wine vinegar

2 teaspoons dried thyme

1 teaspoon celery salt

¼ teaspoon red pepper flakes, or to taste

12 ounces mixed baby greens

In a wok, preferably nonstick, over medium-high heat, heat 2 tablespoons of the oil. Add the garlic and onion and stir-fry for 2 minutes. Add the remaining 2 tablespoons oil, and add the eggplant, zucchini, bell peppers, and tomatoes and their juices and stir-fry for 10 minutes. Reduce the heat to medium, cover, and cook, stirring occasionally, for about 20 minutes, or until the vegetables are tender. If using fresh tomatoes, add ½ cup tomato juice, or as needed, during cooking to keep the vegetables moist. During the last 5 minutes of cooking, stir in the vinegar, thyme, celery salt, and red pepper flakes to taste. Taste and adjust the seasonings as needed.

To serve, mound the mixed baby greens on individual plates and spoon the ratatouille over the greens. Serve warm.

FRAGRANT RED CABBAGE

Braising is a traditional way to cook cabbage, perhaps because it so nicely mellows the vegetable's pungent flavor. A nutritional powerhouse, cabbage provides good doses of vitamin C, vitamin K, and folate.

MAKES 4 SERVINGS

1 small head red cabbage

3 tablespoons unsalted butter

3 tablespoons firmly packed dark brown sugar

⅓ cup cider vinegar

½ cup dried currants

1 cup apple juice

¼ teaspoon ground cinnamon

1 teaspoon fresh marjoram or savory, or ½ teaspoon dried

Salt and freshly ground pepper

Remove the outer leaves of the cabbage and discard. Halve the cabbage, then cut it into shreds. You should have about 6 cups.

In a wok, preferably nonstick, over medium heat, melt the butter. Add the cabbage, brown sugar, vinegar, currants, apple juice, cinnamon, and marjoram. Season with salt and pepper to taste. Cook, stirring occasionally, for 8 to 10 minutes, or until the cabbage is soft. Spoon the cabbage into a serving dish and serve hot.

Note: You can substitute raisins or chopped cooked chestnuts for the currants. In place of the apple juice, you can use apple cider or white or red wine.

CREAMY BLACK RICE PUDDING WITH HAZELNUTS

This combination of comfort food and luxury is irresistible. For a lively contrast in colors and textures, sprinkle some pomegranate seeds over the pudding before serving. Hazelnut syrup is available in specialty-food stores, coffee shops, and some supermarkets.

MAKES 4 TO 6 SERVINGS

2 cups black sticky rice, rinsed

2 cups heavy cream or half-and-half

1 cup milk

½ cup dried cherries or currants

1 tablespoon hazelnut syrup, or to taste

¼ cup firmly packed dark brown sugar

⅓ cup ground hazelnuts for garnishing

Pomegranate seeds for garnishing

Put the rice in a bowl and add enough water to cover by 2 inches. Let stand for at least 5 hours or up to 12 hours. Drain.

Put the rice in a nonstick wok, and add enough water to cover by 2 inches. Bring to a boil over high heat. Reduce the heat to medium, cover, and cook, stirring occasionally and adding more hot water if needed, for 30 minutes, or until the rice is tender but still chewy. Drain.

Return the rice to the wok and add the cream, milk, cherries, hazelnut syrup, and brown sugar. Reduce the heat to medium-low and simmer for about 10 minutes, or until the liquid is almost absorbed. If the pudding is too dry, add a small amount of milk or cream.

Divide the rice pudding among dessert bowls and garnish with the ground hazelnuts and pomegranate seeds. Serve warm.

NECTARINES IN GREEN TEA

*Thanks in part to its purported health benefits, green tea has enjoyed a surge of popularity in this country.
It comes in an array of flavors. In this dessert, green tea lends an intriguing undertone to nectarines.
The fruit tastes great spooned over vanilla or green tea ice cream.*

MAKES 4 SERVINGS

2 cups water

2 to 3 tablespoons honey, or peach jam

¼ teaspoon vanilla extract

3 fruit- or ginger-scented green tea bags

4 medium nectarines, or peeled peaches, halved and pitted

In a wok over high heat, bring the water, 2 tablespoons of the honey, and the vanilla to a boil. Simmer for 1 minute. Remove from the heat and add the tea bags. Steep for 5 minutes.

Remove the tea bags and discard. Taste the liquid and, if desired, add up to 1 tablespoon honey. Set the wok over high heat and boil the liquid for 1 to 2 minutes, or until syrupy.

Add the nectarines to the hot liquid. Reduce the heat to medium-low and simmer for 1 minute, then ladle the nectarines and the liquid into a heatproof glass bowl.

Cover and refrigerate for at least 2 hours or up to 24 hours. Serve chilled.

CHAPTER SEVEN

TAKING UP SMOKING

(AND GRILLING)

STIR-FRYING ON THE GRILL? WHY NOT? WOKS TRADITIONALLY HAVE BEEN USED OVER OPEN OUTDOOR FIRES—AND IN MANY PLACES IN RURAL ASIA, THEY STILL ARE. IN MUCH OF CHINA, EVEN INDOOR COOKING TAKES PLACE ON STOVES FIRED BY WOOD OR COAL. GRILL-WOKKING IS A GREAT WAY TO TAKE YOUR FAVORITE FOODS AND STIR-FRYING TECHNIQUES OUTDOORS, AND IT'S FUN FOR GUESTS TO WATCH. THE RULES ARE THE SAME ONES THAT GOVERN STOVETOP STIR-FRYING: PREPARATION, HEAT, AND ATTENTION. YOU ALSO NEED TO FOLLOW THE RULES FOR GRILLING. LET THE COALS BURN DOWN TO A MEDIUM ASH. TO CHECK, PLACE YOUR HAND, PALM DOWN, ABOUT A HALF INCH ABOVE THE GRILL RACK. YOU SHOULD BE ABLE TO HOLD IT THERE FOR ABOUT 4 SECONDS BEFORE THE HEAT FORCES YOU TO PULL IT AWAY. FOR A CLEAN, HOT FIRE, WE RECOMMEND USING HARDWOOD CHARCOAL, BUT BRIQUETTES WILL ALSO WORK FINE. IF YOU'RE USING A GAS GRILL, CLOSE THE LID AND PREHEAT IT ON HIGH.

All the foods, including side dishes, need to be prepared before you begin grilling. Keep tools, including pot holders, near the grill.

Use a carbon-steel or cast-iron wok for grilling. You can buy special grill woks, which have holes in them to let in more heat from the fire, but a regular wok will work fine. If you don't have a flat-bottomed wok, use the wok ring to support the wok on the grill rack.

This chapter includes a few grill recipes to get you started, but have fun and experiment with other stir-fried recipes on the grill. As long as you let the wok get hot enough, most stir-fries should work as well outside as in. For simplicity's sake, we suggest grill-wokking dishes with no more than five or six ingredients.

It's also easy to smoke foods in a wok, right on the stovetop, without investing in special equipment. Tea, which burns easily and has enough moisture to give off a good amount of pleasantly aromatic smoke, is the traditional smoking medium in Asia. For a change of taste, you can try coffee, as we do in the smoked tofu recipe.

Any metal wok without a nonstick coating is fine for stovetop smoking. Line the wok with aluminum foil to keep the pan's oily finish from absorbing the smoky flavors. There's no need to line the lid, which you can easily wash. Because wok lids often do not fit tightly, we recommend using foil or wet paper towels to seal the perimeter where the lid meets the wok; this will keep the smoke from leaking out.

When you are smoking foods, do not open the lid until the standing time is up, or you may set off your smoke alarm. Run the stove exhaust fan and open a window.

Be sure not to oversmoke foods. There's a fine line between a dish that's pleasantly smoky and one that tastes like old cigarettes. Tofu, in particular, absorbs flavors readily and should be smoked for only a short time.

Wok smoking does not heat foods enough to cook them. If you are smoking meat or poultry, it must be cooked before being smoked. Tofu should be refrigerated immediately after smoking if you aren't going to eat it right away.

VERY LONG GREEN BEANS WITH GROUND BEEF

Long beans are available in Asian markets and some supermarkets. You can use regular green beans instead.

MAKES 4 TO 6 SERVINGS

2 tablespoons soy sauce

2 tablespoons dry white wine

2 tablespoons peanut oil

3 cloves garlic, minced

¾ pound ground lean beef

1 serrano chile, chopped

1 pound long beans or regular green beans

½ cup crushed canned tomatoes, with juice

Salt and freshly ground pepper

In a small bowl, combine the soy sauce and wine.

Preheat a gas grill on high or light a fire in a charcoal grill. When the charcoal is ashen, spread the chunks or briquettes out evenly and set the grill rack in place. Set a wok (and its ring, if needed) on the rack.

When the wok is hot, pour in the oil and heat. Add the garlic, beef, and chile and stir-fry for 3 to 4 minutes, or until the beef is no longer pink. Add the beans and stir-fry for about 2 minutes, or until they are hot and the beef is completely cooked through. Stir in the tomatoes and their juice and mix well. Season with salt and pepper to taste, then stir in the soy sauce mixture. Serve immediately.

GRILL-WOKKED CHICKEN SALAD À LA GRECQUE

The classic combination of garlic, olive oil, and oregano gives poultry a warm, rustic Mediterranean flavor that's perfect for the lazy days of summer. Serve with warm pita bread.

MAKES 4 SERVINGS

3 cloves garlic, minced

⅓ cup olive oil

2 teaspoons minced fresh oregano, or ¾ teaspoon dried

1 pound boneless, skinless chicken breast halves, cut into strips

6 handfuls (about 6 ounces) mixed baby greens

1 large red onion, thinly sliced

¾ cup chopped, drained oil-packed dried tomatoes

4 ounces feta cheese, cut into cubes

¼ cup balsamic vinegar

¼ cup kalamata olives

In a nonreactive bowl or large self-sealing plastic bag, combine the garlic, olive oil, and oregano. Add the chicken and turn to coat with the marinade. Cover the bowl or seal the bag and refrigerate for 4 to 6 hours.

Mound the greens on a platter and arrange the onion slices on top.

Preheat a gas grill on high or light a fire in a charcoal grill. When the charcoal is ashen, spread the chunks or briquettes out evenly and set the grill rack in place. Set a wok (and its ring, if needed) on the rack.

Put the chicken and the marinade in the wok. Stir-fry for 2 to 3 minutes, or until the chicken is no longer pink. Add the tomatoes, cheese, vinegar, and olives. Cook for about 1 minute, or until heated through. Spoon the chicken onto the greens. Serve immediately.

MUSSELS ON THE GRILL

Once upon a time, mussels were considered "poor man's oysters," but now they have come into their own as a delicious seafood. Today's mussels are farm-raised and easy to prepare—just rinse them and snip off any "beards." If you can find it, fresh seaweed adds moisture and a pleasantly briny flavor, and makes for a lovely presentation of the finished dish. Garlic bread and a crisp green salad go just fine with these mussels.

MAKES 4 SERVINGS

Sauce

3 large tomatoes, chopped, with juices

3 tablespoons extra-virgin olive oil

½ cup chopped fresh cilantro

¼ cup capers, with liquid

2 pounds (45 to 50) medium mussels

Fresh seaweed (optional)

To make the sauce: In a bowl, toss the tomatoes and their juices with the oil, cilantro, and capers.

Rinse the mussels under cold running water and snip off any seaweed "beards." Discard any cracked mussels or any that are open and do not close when lightly tapped.

Preheat a gas grill on high or light a fire in a charcoal grill. When the charcoal is ashen, spread the chunks or briquettes out evenly and set the grill rack in place. Set a wok (and its ring, if needed) on the rack.

Arrange the seaweed, if using, in the wok and top with the mussels. Cover and cook for 4 to 5 minutes, or until the mussels open. Discard any that do not open. Transfer the mussels and seaweed to a platter. Sprinkle the mussels with the sauce and serve.

STIR-FRIED POUND CAKE WITH STRAWBERRIES

Feel free to substitute other berries, depending on what's in season.
We're especially fond of blackberries with blackberry or vanilla ice cream.

MAKES 4 SERVINGS

2 heaping cups sliced strawberries

3 tablespoons Grand Marnier

3 tablespoons unsalted butter

6 slices pound cake, cut into 1-inch cubes

4 scoops strawberry ice cream

In a bowl, combine the strawberries and Grand Marnier.

Preheat a gas grill on high or light a fire in a charcoal grill. When the charcoal is ashen, spread the chunks or briquettes out evenly and set the grill rack in place. Set a wok (and its ring, if needed) on the rack.

Melt the butter in the wok. Add the pound cake and stir-fry for a few seconds, or until it begins to turn golden brown. Watch carefully so it doesn't burn.

Working quickly, divide the cake among 4 dessert dishes. Top each portion with a scoop of ice cream. Garnish with the berries and serve immediately.

TEA-SMOKED CHICKEN WITH FIG CONFIT

Wok smoking does not cook foods but merely flavors them, which is why the chicken must be steamed first. Although fig confit is not part of the traditional Chinese smoked dish, its sweetness provides a lovely counterpoint to smoked foods. Try it with pork or turkey as well. This dish can be served cold or at room temperature, so keep it in mind for your next party. The smoked chicken is also good in a salad of mixed greens and dried cranberries.

MAKES 6 SERVINGS

3½ pounds chicken, in serving pieces

½ cup firmly packed light brown sugar

¼ cup dark tea leaves, such as black tea or orange pekoe

1 cup chopped fresh cilantro

Fig Confit (recipe follows) for serving

Fill a wok one-half to two-thirds full of water and bring to a boil over high heat. Reduce the heat to medium and fit an oiled steamer rack in the wok, or invert a custard cup or other heatproof cup in the wok and set an oiled heatproof plate atop it. Arrange the chicken on the rack or plate, cover, and steam for 45 minutes to 1 hour, depending on the size of the chicken pieces. For example, thick chicken legs will need to steam for about 1 hour, or until cooked through. Check once or twice during steaming and add more boiling water if needed.

Transfer the chicken to a platter and pat dry with paper towels.

Clean and dry the wok thoroughly and line with heavy-duty aluminum foil. Sprinkle the brown sugar and tea leaves on the foil. Set a metal rack large enough to hold the chicken in the wok. It should sit at least 2 inches above the sugar and tea.

Place the chicken on the rack and cover the wok tightly. Turn the heat to high and smoke the chicken for 20 minutes. Remove from the heat but do not uncover the wok. Let stand for about 15 minutes, or until you no longer see wisps of smoke. Transfer the chicken to a serving dish. Sprinkle with cilantro and serve warm or cold, accompanied by the fig confit. If you prefer, you can remove the chicken from the bones and slice it.

FIG CONFIT

MAKES 1½ CUPS

3 tablespoons unsalted butter

½ cup thinly sliced onion

6 to 8 fresh figs, stemmed and quartered, enough to make 1 cup

⅓ cup golden raisins

3 tablespoons firmly packed light brown sugar

2 tablespoons rice vinegar

In a wok over medium heat, melt the butter. Add the onion and stir-fry for 4 to 5 minutes, or until tender. Add the figs and stir-fry for 1 minute. Add the raisins, brown sugar, and vinegar and cook, stirring, for 2 to 3 minutes, or until the sugar is melted.

Spoon the confit into a small bowl. Serve warm, or cover and refrigerate. Stir before serving.

COFFEE-SMOKED TOFU

We were introduced to coffee smoking by a segment on the Iron Chef, *the entertaining show on the Food Network that is Japan's culinary equivalent of wrestling. Challenger Chef Sakai, who runs an Italian restaurant in Tokyo, smoked eels over coffee beans and brown sugar, an idea that intrigued us. Sure enough, coffee produces a good smoke that adds a bittersweet note to foods. We admit that eels don't grab us, but coffee is a great smoking medium for tofu, chicken, and shellfish. If you prefer, you can bow to tradition and use tea leaves instead of coffee beans. The smoked tofu can be served plain, but it tastes best pan-fried in a little oil, or brushed lightly with oil and grilled.*

MAKES 4 SERVINGS

3 tablespoons soy sauce

1½ tablespoons maple syrup, or light unsulphured molasses

¼ teaspoon freshly ground pepper

1 pound extra-firm tofu (see Note)

¼ cup firmly packed light brown sugar

¼ cup whole coffee beans, or black tea leaves

In a large, shallow nonreactive dish, combine the soy sauce, maple syrup, and pepper.

Drain the tofu and cut it lengthwise into 8 slices. Line a colander with a single thickness of paper towels, set the tofu in the colander, and let drain for 30 minutes. Place the tofu in the soy sauce mixture, turning to coat with the marinade. If the slices won't fit in a single layer, overlap them slightly. Cover and refrigerate for at least 4 hours or up to 24 hours, turning the slices once or twice to make sure they're coated with marinade.

Line a wok with heavy-duty aluminum foil. Sprinkle the brown sugar and coffee beans on the foil. Set an oiled metal rack in the wok.

Remove the tofu from the marinade and pat dry with paper towels. Arrange on the rack, overlapping the slices slightly. Cover the wok tightly and turn the heat to medium-high. As soon as you see wisps of smoke rising around the edges of the lid, reduce the heat to medium and smoke the tofu for 2 minutes. Remove from the heat but do not uncover the wok. Let stand for 5 to 7 minutes, or until you no longer see wisps of smoke.

Eat immediately, or transfer the tofu to a plate and refrigerate.

Note: The tofu sold in tubs works best in this recipe. Silken-style tofu (the kind that comes in shelf-stable packages) may fall apart.

BASIC TECHNIQUES AND RECIPES

CONDIMENTS, GARNISHES, AND RICE

DEEP-FRIED ONIONS, GARLIC, OR SHALLOTS

Cut the onions, garlic, or shallots lengthwise into thin slices or fine strips. In a small wok or heavy saucepan over medium-high heat, heat about 1 cup of vegetable or peanut oil. Add the onions, garlic, or shallots and fry for a few seconds, or until golden. Do not let them turn dark brown. Using a slotted spoon, transfer to paper towels to drain, then cover loosely with a paper towel and refrigerate until serving. If the onions lose their crispness, put them in a pie tin and reheat in a 350°F oven for 5 to 10 minutes, or until crisp. *Note: You must use clean, fresh oil for frying; if the oil is dirty, the black bits will cling to the onions. After frying, discard the oil, which will have a strong smell. Instead of making your own, you can buy packaged fried onions or shallots in some Asian markets.*

GREEN ONION (SCALLION) BRUSHES

These pretty garnishes are easy to make. Trim off all but 2 to 3 inches of the green top of each green onion. Using a small, sharp knife, make a lengthwise slit 1 to 1½ inches long in the white bulb. Give the onion a quarter turn and make another slit. Repeat this procedure with the green part. Place the onions in a shallow bowl of cold water and refrigerate for at least 1 hour, or until the slit ends curl up.

ASIAN OMELETTE

Rolled and cut into strips, this thin omelette adds flavor and color to dishes ranging from pad Thai to fried rice. Beat 1 egg. Pour into a nonstick skillet or wok, twirling the pan to cover the bottom with a thin coating of egg. As soon as it is set, remove from the pan with a spatula and let cool. Roll the omelette up and cut crosswise into thin strips. Refrigerate until needed.

ASIAN PANCAKES

These classic pancakes are used in dishes such as mu shu pork.
Instead of making your own pancakes, you can substitute flour tortillas, which are thicker.

MAKES 12 PANCAKES

2½ cups all-purpose flour, plus more as needed

½ teaspoon salt

1 cup boiling water

1 tablespoon vegetable shortening

Dark sesame oil for brushing

In the large bowl of an electric mixer, combine the flour and salt on low speed. Increase the speed to medium and add the boiling water in a slow steady stream, mixing well. Mix in the shortening. Turn the dough out onto a lightly floured pastry cloth, gather together, and knead until smooth. Let the dough stand for 15 minutes.

Divide the dough into 12 equal pieces and shape each one into a ball. Press each ball into a circle and brush with sesame oil. Press 1 circle of dough on top of a second one, oiled sides together. Using a rolling pin, roll out into a circle 4½ to 5 inches in diameter, sprinkling with additional flour as needed. Repeat with the remaining dough circles.

Heat a wok over medium-high heat. Place 1 double pancake in the center of the wok and cook for about 30 seconds, or until it begins to brown on one side. Turn it over and continue cooking for about 30 seconds, or until the other side begins to brown.

Remove the double pancake from the wok and, working quickly, separate it into 2 pancakes. Repeat with the remaining pancakes. Serve warm.

To make ahead of time: These pancakes can be prepared in advance and frozen for up to 6 months. Stack them with sheets of plastic wrap or waxed paper between them, then wrap in plastic wrap or aluminum foil. To reheat, place 6 pancakes at a time on a plate, cover loosely with plastic wrap, and microwave for about 10 seconds, or until warm. Or steam them in a wok for a few minutes until warm.

PERFECT RICE

No doubt about it, the best way to cook rice is with a rice cooker. This electric appliance, which cooks the grains over low heat and shuts off when the water has been absorbed, is indispensable if you cook a lot of rice. Follow the manufacturer's directions. You may need to adjust the water level a bit, depending on the rice variety. If you don't have a rice cooker, follow these tips for making perfect rice:

Use a heavy pan. We prefer enameled cast iron, but a heavy nonstick wok works fine. A thin pan will cause the rice to scorch.

Use low heat and always gently simmer, never boil, rice. Essentially, you're steaming it.

Don't peek more than once and only then near the end of the cooking time. You'll let steam escape.

Although you'll often see instructions for cooking 1 cup long-grain rice in 2 cups water, that's really too much water. For jasmine rice (the long-grain variety we prefer as our all-purpose rice), 1⅔ cups to 1¾ cups water usually works best. Asian cooks have a rule of thumb—or maybe we should call it a rule of knuckle—for rice: The water above the rice should come up about as high as the first joint on your index finger. The larger the amount of rice, the less the amount of water needed, proportionately speaking.

Short-grain rices require much more water. For example, sticky (glutinous) rice is usually cooked in enough water to cover the rice by 2 inches.

Although Asian cultures traditionally rinse rice, we don't recommend it. Modern rice is coated with a mixture of B vitamins and iron. When you rinse enriched rice, you pour vitamins down the drain.

Sticky rice is an exception. It must be rinsed, then soaked for several hours or overnight before being steamed. And true basmati rice from India is soaked in cold water to cover for 20 to 30 minutes. The rice is then cooked in the soaking water (plus some fresh water if needed) to retain flavor and nutrients.

If you don't have a rice cooker, try one of these cooking methods for long-grain rice:

Steamer method: Put 2 cups rice in a pan that is shallow enough to fit inside a bamboo steamer with the lid, or on a steamer rack with the wok lid in place (use a large cake pan if you have to). Fill a wok one-half to two-thirds full of water and bring to a boil over high heat. Ladle 2½ to 2⅔ cups of the boiling water into the pan with the rice. The water should come about ¾ inch above the rice. Add ½ teaspoon salt if desired. Replenish the water in the wok if needed so the wok is at least half full of water. Fit the steamer or steamer rack in the wok, and place the pan in or on the steamer. Cover the pan loosely with aluminum foil, and cover the steamer or the wok. Reduce the heat to medium.

CONTINUED →

Steam for 20 to 25 minutes for white rice, 45 to 55 minutes for brown rice, or until the rice has absorbed the water. Check the water level in the wok after 20 minutes of cooking to make sure it's not too low. Remove the rice pan from the steamer and let stand, covered, for 5 minutes. Fluff and serve.

Stovetop method: Use a nonstick wok or other heavy pan. Bring 1⅔ to 1¾ cups water and ½ teaspoon salt, if desired, to a boil. Stir in 1 cup rice. Reduce the heat to very low, cover the pan tightly, and cook for 15 to 20 minutes for white rice, 45 to 50 minutes for brown rice, or until the rice has absorbed the water. Remove from the heat and let stand, covered, for 5 minutes. Fluff and serve.

Check the rice as soon as you remove it from the heat. If it is still too chewy, stir in ¼ cup boiling water and let stand for 5 minutes.

SWEET SOY DIPPING SAUCE

With minor variations, this sauce can be used with a range of dishes, from Korean to Chinese. It's a great accompaniment to steamed dumplings or fried foods such as tempura or wontons. If you use dark soy sauce (a blend of well-aged soy sauce and molasses), you can omit the sugar.

MAKES ABOUT ½ CUP

¼ cup soy sauce

2 teaspoons sugar or light molasses

2 to 4 teaspoons Chinese cooking wine, sherry, or mirin

¼ cup chicken broth, dashi, or water

Grated fresh ginger or horseradish, or finely chopped green onion (optional)

In a small nonreactive bowl, mix the soy sauce with the sugar and wine to taste, stirring to dissolve the sugar. Stir in the broth. Add a little grated ginger, if using. Cover and refrigerate. Bring to room temperature before serving.

Variation: For a more piquant dipping sauce that's great with steamed vegetables, add 1 to 2 teaspoons rice vinegar.

NUOC CHAM

No Vietnamese table is complete without this pungent condiment. The ingredients vary, but fish sauce and vinegar are always included. Westerners tend to prefer it a bit on the sweet side, so we use a little more sugar. Serve with spring rolls, rice, or dumplings.

MAKES ABOUT ½ CUP

3 tablespoons Southeast Asian fish sauce

4 to 6 teaspoons sugar

3 tablespoons rice vinegar, or fresh lime juice

1 clove garlic, finely minced

Red pepper flakes

2 tablespoons shredded carrot or cabbage (optional)

Minced fresh cilantro (optional)

In a small nonreactive bowl or a clean jar, combine the fish sauce, sugar to taste, vinegar, garlic, red pepper flakes to taste, and carrot and cilantro, if using. Stir or shake until the sugar dissolves. Add water if needed until the sauce is to your taste. Cover and refrigerate until ready to serve. The sauce will keep up to 1 month in the refrigerator.

SPICY KETCHUP

*Tomato ketchup has been produced commercially in the United States since 1876,
but it began as a British home recipe in the late eighteenth century and found its way to the colonies.
Make this recipe in the fall when you have an abundance of garden tomatoes.*

MAKES ABOUT 2¼ CUPS

12 large ripe tomatoes, seeded and chopped, juices reserved

1 small onion, minced

1 small red bell pepper, seeded, deribbed, and minced

½ cup cider or tarragon vinegar

2 teaspoons powdered mustard

½ teaspoon salt

½ teaspoon ground allspice

½ teaspoon peeled, minced fresh ginger

¼ teaspoon freshly ground pepper

¼ teaspoon paprika

In a wok, preferably nonstick, or medium heavy-bottomed saucepan over medium-high heat, combine the tomatoes and their juices, onion, and bell pepper. Simmer, stirring often, for 20 minutes, or until soft. Transfer to a bowl.

Rinse out the wok and wipe it dry. Push the vegetables through a strainer and return the puree to the wok. Mix in the vinegar, mustard, salt, allspice, ginger, pepper, and paprika. Simmer over medium-low heat, stirring occasionally, for 20 minutes, or until the ketchup thickens. Taste and adjust the seasonings. Let cool.

Spoon the ketchup into a bowl or jar, cover, and refrigerate until ready to serve. Stir before serving. This is best used within 1 week.

BASIC TECHNIQUES

BUTTERFLYING SHRIMP

To butterfly shrimp, use a small, sharp knife to cut down the back of the shrimp, cutting partway, not all the way, through it. If the shrimp has a shell, peel it off. Remove the vein down the back, if present. Then gently press open the shrimp so it is slightly flattened.

GRATING CITRUS ZEST

Remove the zest with a citrus zester, or grate the citrus fruit on the small holes of a regular grater. Use only the outermost, colored part of the rind, not the bitter white pith.

RECONSTITUTING MUSHROOMS

Dried mushrooms such as shiitakes must be reconstituted before being used in cooking. Soak the mushrooms in hot water to cover for 20 to 30 minutes, or until pliable. *Note: Since hot tap water is more likely to contain lead and other undesirable chemicals, it is best to heat cold water in the microwave or on the stovetop before soaking porous foods such as mushrooms or noodles.* Or, soak them in cold water and add 5 to 10 minutes to the soaking time.

SOAKING NOODLES

Because they lack gluten (the protein that gives wheat pasta its chewiness), rice noodles and bean threads may fall apart if they are boiled for too long. So they often are soaked until pliable, then quickly cooked in stir-fries and other dishes. Soaking also helps rid rice noodles of some of their starch, making them less sticky.

Soak noodles in hot water to cover for about 15 minutes, or until pliable. (See the note regarding hot tap water under Reconstituting Mushrooms, page 207.) Alternatively, you can soak noodles in cold water for about 30 minutes or in boiling water for 1 to 2 minutes.

PREPARING FRESH HERBS AND SPICES

CHILES

Halve the chiles lengthwise, and remove and discard the seeds. (For more heat, keep the seeds.) You may wish to wear rubber gloves when handling chiles to keep the oils from getting on your hands. If you don't wear gloves, wash your hands thoroughly after chopping chiles, and do not rub your eyes for at least an hour or two afterward.

GARLIC

To peel fresh garlic, whack the clove with the flat side of a heavy knife. The peel should loosen and come off easily. Then chop the garlic with the knife. For larger amounts of garlic, a garlic press or a mini–food chopper is handy.

GINGER

When we mince ginger, we peel it first. When we grate it, we don't bother. Use a ceramic ginger grater or the small holes of a regular grater.

FRESH HERBS

Strip the leaves from the stems and discard the stems. To chop or mince large-leafed herbs such as basil, roll the leaves up tightly, cigar-fashion, then cut crosswise into strips. Use the strips as is or chop into smaller pieces.

TOASTING NUTS

Toasting nuts brings out their natural oils, enhancing their flavor. You can toast a small amount of nuts in a small skillet or wok. Heat the pan over medium heat, add the nuts, and cook, stirring or tossing frequently, until they just turn golden and give off a rich, toasted smell. This will take only a couple of minutes. Watch carefully so they do not burn. To toast a larger quantity of nuts, spread them out in a single layer on a baking sheet and toast in a 350°F oven for 5 to 10 minutes, or until they give off a rich, toasted aroma.

GLOSSARY AND GUIDE TO INGREDIENTS

ANISE: See fennel (the vegetable) or star anise (the spice).

BABY BOK CHOY: Regular bok choy, a relative of the cabbage with wide, creamy stalks and dark green leaves, is readily available in supermarkets. Baby bok choy, a smaller version, is harder to find. Look in Asian markets and natural-food stores. This lovely jade-colored vegetable is worth seeking out. It has a milder flavor than its larger cousin, and the smaller leaves can be cooked whole for an especially pretty dish. Larger leaves (longer than about 4 inches) can be halved lengthwise.

BLACK BEANS, BLACK BEAN SAUCE: Fermented and salted soybeans are a staple of Chinese cooking. They taste a bit like soy sauce but have a deeper flavor. They're traditionally paired with seafood and with assertive vegetables such as broccoli and asparagus but go well with a wide variety of foods. The beans themselves, plain or flavored, may be sold in plastic bags in Asian markets, although they are increasingly hard to find. It's much more common to see black bean sauce in jars, especially black bean and garlic sauce. A little of this strongly flavored paste goes a long way.

CHILE PASTE: Made of ground red chiles and oil and sometimes flavored with garlic, this paste is found in Asian markets and some supermarkets.

CHINESE FIVE-SPICE POWDER: Traditionally, this Chinese blend contained five spices, although modern versions often contain more. The powder generally includes at least five of the following spices: cinnamon, star anise, pepper, fennel, ginger, licorice, and cloves. A key ingredient in roasted duck and simmered dishes, Chinese five-spice powder is available in Asian markets and most supermarkets.

CURRY PASTE: This Thai seasoning is commonly used in coconut-based curries. The most popular varieties are green, made from fresh chiles, and red, made from dried red chiles. The chiles are ground into a paste with other herbs and spices, which usually include coriander, garlic, shallots, and lemongrass. Although curry pastes taste best made fresh, we use bottled sauces for the sake of convenience. Curry pastes are available in Asian markets. Look for a brand that contains quality ingredients, with no fillers.

CURRY POWDER: A British invention meant to evoke the multispiced cuisine of India, curry powder is used almost everywhere in southern Asia except India. The powder derives its yellow color from turmeric, and cheap curry powders are made mostly of that rather bland spice. Good curry powders, which come in mild and hot versions, contain a higher proportion of such fragrant spices as ginger, coriander, cumin, cardamom, chiles, and cinnamon.

DASHI: The basic Japanese stock, dashi is made from seaweed and dried fish (bonito) steeped in water. Powdered dashi mixes are sold in stores that stock Japanese ingredients.

DRIED SHRIMP: Just what the name says: these are small shrimp that have been dried. They are sold in the shell or peeled. Soak and chop them before using. Like the anchovies in a Caesar salad, they add a subtle but important flavor to many Asian dishes, such as dumplings and curries. Dried shrimp are available in Latino and Asian markets and many supermarkets. Southeast Asian markets also sell dried shrimp powder and paste.

EDAMAME (ED-AH-MAH-MAY): Green soybeans (edamame is their Japanese name) are sold in pods or shelled. They are available frozen and occasionally fresh in natural-food stores, many Asian markets, and some supermarkets. A popular snack in Japan, edamame are delicious lightly steamed or boiled and eaten as is, with a bit of salt or soy sauce.

FENNEL: The seeds (actually fruits) are sold as a spice and the bulbs and stalks are sold as a fresh vegetable that many supermarkets erroneously label "anise." The bulb is cut up and used in stir-fries, salads, and sautés. The stems and leaves are good for flavoring sauces and soups. Although fennel is traditionally associated with Italian cooking, its anise flavor makes it ideal for many Asian and cross-cultural dishes.

FISH SAUCE: Called *nam pla* in Thailand and *nuoc mam* in Vietnam, this thin, odorous sauce made from fermented anchovies, water, and salt is essential to Southeast Asian cookery. It's found in markets that carry Southeast Asian ingredients and, increasingly, in supermarkets. *Nuoc cham* (see recipe, page 205), an essential table condiment in Vietnam, is a mixture of fish sauce, vinegar, sugar, and seasonings.

FIVE-SPICE: See Chinese five-spice powder.

GARAM MASALA: This fragrant blend of roasted spices is used in the cooking of northern India. The spices vary according to the cook (or manufacturer) but often include several of the following: cardamom, pepper, cumin, coriander, and cinnamon. You can find ready-made garam masala in markets that carry Indian ingredients and in some supermarkets.

GREEN ONIONS: Technically, they're scallions, not green onions (the latter have a definite bulb), but since the two are so similar and supermarkets label them "green onions," we do, too. Unless otherwise directed, use the white parts and 1 to 2 inches of the green tops. To make scallion brushes, see page 201.

HOISIN SAUCE: A thick, dark, sweet Chinese sauce, hoisin is made from soybeans, sugar, vinegar, garlic, and other ingredients, typically flour, chile, sesame oil, and artificial or natural red coloring. It can be used sparingly as a condiment, but is also good in stir-fries and simmered dishes, and as a paste for marinating roasted or grilled meats. We recommend buying hoisin from an Asian market, where you'll have a choice of several brands of varying quality. Supermarkets frequently carry only one brand, often of inferior quality.

LEMONGRASS: This herb, which looks a bit like a scallion that grew up in a tough neighborhood, hides its heart under several layers of woody, light green–purplish foliage. It's a key ingredient in Southeast Asian cuisines, and you can find it in Asian food stores or in many supermarkets. Lemongrass is available both fresh and dried, though it tastes better fresh. To prepare it, peel off the woody outer leaves until you reach the creamy-colored, tender inner stem, which can be chopped or minced. The woody parts can be frozen and used to flavor soups and sauces.

LOTUS ROOT: The rhizome of the lotus, a relative of the water lily, lotus root has channels running through it that show up as attractive holes when it is sliced crosswise. It is sold dried in Asian markets, but for tempura, use fresh lotus root, which is sometimes available in Asian markets, natural-food stores, and supermarkets. Cut into thin slices and deep-fried, this creamy-colored, buttery-textured root is irresistible. It is also good in soups and salads. If using lotus root raw or steaming it, soak it in water and lemon juice to keep it from discoloring.

MIRIN: See wines for cooking.

NOODLES AND WRAPPERS

BEAN THREADS: Also called cellophane or glass noodles because they're transparent when cooked, bean threads are made from the starch of the mung bean. They're used in noodle dishes and as an ingredient in fillings for dumplings and spring rolls. They can be soaked or boiled before using.

DUMPLING WRAPPERS: Many supermarkets carry both square (wonton wrappers) and round (dumpling or gyoza wrappers) shapes in the refrigerated section, usually near the tofu. Though not as light as homemade wrappers, they're very convenient. They dry out rapidly once unwrapped, so cover them with a damp cloth until ready to use.

RICE PAPER WRAPPERS: Similar to rice noodles, rice paper wrappers are as thin as glass and almost as translucent. They are very fragile. Soak them in warm water to soften, then wrap them around various fillings. They can be eaten raw in fresh spring rolls or fried to golden crispness. Sold in Asian markets, rice paper wrappers come in 8-inch (the most common size) and 6-inch diameters.

RICE STICKS (NOODLES): Made of rice flour and water, these noodles come in various widths, ranging from very fine noodles that are usually deep-fried to noodles ⅛- to ¼-inch thick that are good for stir-fries, such as Pad Thai (page 89). Rice sticks are readily available in Asian markets and some supermarkets. They should be soaked to soften them for stir-frying or other quick cooking.

WHEAT FLOUR NOODLES: Made of plain flour and water or flour and egg, these noodles come in extra-thin widths such as vermicelli, which are used in dishes such as ramen; wider noodles are used in stir-fry dishes such as lo mein. They're available fresh, dried, or frozen in Asian markets and many supermarkets. Generally, the fresh or dried pasta found in the supermarket makes a fine substitute.

OYSTER SAUCE: Not to be confused with fish sauce, this dark, thick, slightly sweet sauce is made of oysters, water, salt, and cornstarch. It's widely used as an all-purpose sauce in Chinese cooking and is especially good with slightly pungent vegetables such as broccoli. Oyster sauce is sold in Asian markets and some supermarkets.

PANCETTA: An Italian bacon that is cured with spices and salt but not smoked, pancetta is used to flavor a variety of dishes. If you cannot find it, substitute a top-quality smoked bacon.

PARMESAN CHEESE: When possible, use the real thing, Parmigiano-Reggiano imported from Italy. Its nutty-sweet flavor leaves its imitators far behind. However, a decent domestic Parmesan will suffice. Grate it yourself, or buy it already grated in the refrigerated cheese section of the supermarket. Be sure to use fresh, not canned, Parmesan.

RED PEPPER FLAKES, CRUSHED RED PEPPER: Labeled one or the other, depending on the brand, this hot seasoning is made from dried red chiles that are crushed to make a flaky spice. It's widely available in supermarkets.

RICE AND RICE FLOUR

LONG-GRAIN RICE: The grains cook up long, fluffy, and separate. Long-grain rice is available in both regular varieties—the familiar boxed supermarket brands—and aromatic rices, which give off a nutty, popcorn fragrance as they cook. Long-grain rices are good all-purpose rices, whether served plain or with other ingredients. The two most popular aromatic rices are basmati, which swells lengthwise during cooking and becomes dry, almost lacy, and jasmine, which is a bit softer and stickier (ideal for eating with chopsticks). Jasmine is the all-purpose rice we use the most.

SHORT-GRAIN RICES: These are starchier and absorb more liquid, making them ideal for dishes such as rice cakes and puddings where you want the rice grains to stick together. Arborio, a fat, short-grain rice of Italian heritage, absorbs a lot of liquid and gives off starch to make a creamy sauce. It is used primarily for risottos. On the other side of the world is glutinous rice, also called waxy, sweet, or sticky rice. Sticky rice, whole or ground, is used primarily to make stuffings, rice cakes, dumplings, and puddings. It comes in both white and black. The black tastes somewhat nuttier and cooks into a lovely purple-black hue.

PARBOILED OR CONVERTED RICE: Parboiling is a technique in which the rice is soaked under pressure, steamed, and dried. This gelatinizes the starch and ensures the grains stay separate when cooked. Converted rice retains more nutrients than regular white rice and is good for salads.

RICE FLOUR: Rice is also ground into flour, which is used in dumplings, noodles, and tempura batter. Glutinous or sweet rice flour is made from glutinous rice.

RICE VINEGAR: This mild vinegar is brewed from rice. Aged rice vinegar, available in some Asian markets, has a wonderfully mellow, deep flavor. Much of the rice vinegar sold these days also includes sugar and salt. Check the label before buying it.

ROCK SUGAR: This lumpy, hard, amber-colored crystallized mixture of sugar and water is traditionally used in "red-cooked" dishes (those simmered in a soy sauce–based liquid) to flavor the sauce and make it shine. Rock sugar is available in Asian markets. You can substitute regular or brown sugar.

SESAME OIL: Sesame seeds and oil are used widely around the world. Sesame oil comes in two varieties, a light-colored oil (often heavily processed) and a dark oil made of toasted seeds. We call for the latter in this book because of the rich flavor it adds to dishes. Toasted sesame oil is not suitable for frying except in small amounts mixed with other oils.

SESAME SEEDS: Sesame seeds range in color from pearl to black. The pearl-colored (white) seeds are the most commonly used type in North America, where they flavor everything from bagels to salads. The black seeds are popular in Japan and some other Asian countries. The white seeds are available in supermarkets. The black seeds are available in Asian markets and some supermarkets. Sesame seeds and oil go rancid quickly and should be refrigerated.

SHRIMP PASTE: See dried shrimp.

SOY SAUCE: Go beyond the two brands carried by every super-market, and you'll discover a world of soy sauces that vary widely in strength, color, and, most importantly, quality. At its best, soy sauce is a complexly flavored, nutritious condiment (though high in sodium). At its worst, it's bottled, colored hydrolyzed vegetable protein. Real soy sauce is made of roasted soybean meal and grain (often wheat), combined with salt water, a bacterium (lactobacillus), and yeast. It's aged until it reaches the right color, consistency, and flavor. Most commercially produced soy sauce is aged for a few months. Premium soy sauces may be aged for several years. Asian markets carry the widest variety of soy sauce brands and styles.

Nuances aside, soy sauce falls into two basic categories: LIGHT AND DARK. Light (regular) soy sauce is the one most of us are familiar with and is sold in most supermarkets. (This should not be confused with the reduced-sodium soy sauce labeled "light.") Dark soy sauce, which is aged longer, has molasses added to deepen the flavor and color. Many Asian recipes call for a combination of light and dark soy sauces. But for ease of preparation, we use only the light version.

STAR ANISE: Shaped like its namesake, this pretty, eight-pointed pod comes from an evergreen that grows in China and northern Vietnam. It is not related to European anise. Usually added whole to dishes, it imparts a pleasant licorice flavor and is a key ingredient in Chinese five-spice powder. Star anise is sold in Asian markets.

TAMARI: Available in natural-food stores and some Asian markets, tamari is soy sauce that contains no wheat.

TOFU: Also known as soybean curd, tofu is made much like cheese: Cultures are added to soybean "milk" to create solids, which are drained and pressed into cakes. Its beany blandness and porous texture allow it to absorb the flavors of the other ingredients it's cooked with. Tofu is sold in small water-filled tubs or shelf-stable aseptic packages in supermarkets, Asian stores, and natural-food stores. The aseptically packaged tofu has a silky, custard-style texture, while the tub tofu is firmer. You can buy tofu in a variety of flavors and styles, including baked and fried. Freshness is paramount. Pay attention to the expiration dates, refrigerate promptly, and toss it if it smells sour.

TOMATILLOS: These relatives of the tomato look like small green or yellow tomatoes in papery husks. Pleasantly tart, they are most often used green in both raw and cooked sauces. To prepare them, remove the husk. The husked tomatillos will be slightly sticky. They may be chopped raw for a *salsa cruda* or cooked in a green chile sauce.

WINES FOR COOKING

Although the general rule is to cook with the same wine you'll serve with the meal, you may not be planning to serve wine if you're preparing Asian food. Asian wines are usually rice-based and don't taste much like their grape-based Western counterparts. If you do prefer to use a dry white wine in Asian cooking, we suggest a dry Riesling.

MIRIN: This is a sweet Japanese cooking wine. The best wine, naturally brewed *hon-mirin,* is found in Asian markets. *Aji-mirin,* available in supermarkets, contains wine, salt, and corn syrup and can be used in a pinch. Sake (or a very dry white wine) and a bit of sugar, or a fairly sweet Riesling, is an acceptable substitute for mirin.

SHAOXING *(SHAO-HSING, HUA TIAO)*: A Chinese rice wine from Shaoxing in Zhejiang province, it looks and tastes a lot like sherry, though the wine designed for cooking is salted. It's readily found in Chinese markets, but dry sherry makes a decent substitute.

SOURCES OF EQUIPMENT

AND INGREDIENTS

ASIAFOODS.COM
28 Damrell Street
South Boston, MA 02127
(877) 902-0841
Fax: (617) 269-7007
www.asiafoods.com
Online pan-Asian market, with an emphasis on Chinese ingredients.

CHEF'S CATALOG
P.O. Box 620048
Dallas, TX 75262-0048
(800) 884-CHEF
Fax: (972) 401-6400
www.chefscatalog.com
Stir-fry pans from various manufacturers as well as woks for the grill.

ETHNIC GROCER
(866) 4ETHNIC
www.ethnicgrocer.com
*Online emporium of fresh and packaged foodstuffs from fifteen
countries, including Italy, Mexico, Korea, Japan, China, Thailand,
Vietnam, and India. (Order online or by phone only.)*

IRON WORKS COMPANY STORE
Ironworks, Inc.
P.O. Box 609
Springhill, LA 71075
(800) 811-9890
Fax: (318) 994-3231
www.theironworks.com
*Round-bottomed heavy-gauge carbon-steel woks in sizes from
12 to 28 inches in diameter. Also cast-iron woks, wok sets, and
wok accessories.*

JOYCE CHEN, INC.
6 Fortune Drive
Billerica, MA 01821
(978) 671-9500
Fax: (978) 671-9559
www.joycechen.com
*Round- and flat-bottomed nonstick, carbon-steel, and cast-iron woks,
plus steamers and accessories. No direct ordering by consumers, but
Web site lists stores (both brick-and-mortar and online) that carry
Joyce Chen cookware.*

LUNDBERG FAMILY FARMS
5370 Church Street
P.O. Box 369
Richvale, CA 95974-0369
(530) 882-4551
Fax: (530) 882-4500
www.lundberg.com
*Organically grown brown rice and rice products, specialty rices and
rice mixes, and rice cookers. Products are widely available in
natural-foods stores and some supermarkets, and can be ordered
in bulk directly from Lundberg.*

PACIFIC RIM WOKS AND PACIFIC RIM GOURMET
i-Clipse, Inc.
4905 Morena Boulevard, Suite 1313
San Diego, CA 92117
(800) 910-WOKS
Fax: (858) 274-9018
www.pacificrim-woks.com and www.pacificrim-gourmet.com
*Round- and flat-bottomed carbon-steel woks from 12 to 20 inches
in diameter, cast-iron woks, and electric woks. Also sells bamboo
steamers, clay pots, and Asian foodstuffs.*

PENZEY'S SPICES
P.O. Box 924
Brookfield, WI 53008
(800) 741-7787
Fax: (262) 785-7678
www.penzeys.com
Purveyor of a wide variety of spices, herbs, and spice-and-herb mixes, including curry powder, Vietnamese cinnamon, and Chinese five-spice powder.

PEOPLES WOODS
75 Mill Street
Cumberland, RI 02864
(800) 729-5800
Fax: (401) 725-0006
www.peopleswoods.com
Makers and purveyors of Nature's Own pure hardwood charcoal.

RICESELECT
RiceTec, Inc.
1925 FM 2917
Alvin, TX 77511
(800) 232-RICE
www.riceselect.com
Texas-grown sushi-, superfino-, basmati-, and jasmine-style rices. Widely available in retail stores or in mix-and-match gift packs from RiceSelect.

TAYLOR & NG
170 Rutledge Street
San Francisco, CA 94110-5342
(415) 643-6810
Fax: (415) 643-6859
www.taylorandng.com
San Francisco–based seller of many of the woks found in Chinese markets everywhere, including traditional and preseasoned carbon-steel woks and accessories. Also sells mail order.

THAIGROCER
1430 N. Bosworth, Floor 7
Chicago, IL 60622
(773) 988-8424
Fax: (773) 871-3969
www.thaigrocer.com
A wide variety of Thai and other Southeast Asian ingredients, including brown jasmine rice and black sweet sticky rice. Sells mail order.

BIBLIOGRAPHY

Bittman, Mark.
How to Cook Everything. New York: Macmillan, 1998.

Canola Information Service.
"Canola Oil Frying Tips." World Wide Web,
accessed December 20, 2000, at http://www.canolainfo.org.

Chen, Helen.
Helen Chen's Chinese Home Cooking. New York: Hearst Books, 1994.

Corriher, Shirley.
Cookwise. New York: William Morrow and Company, 1997.

Cost, Bruce.
Bruce Cost's Asian Ingredients.
New York: William Morrow and Company, 1988.

Dornbusch, Jane.
"Savoring Soy: When It Comes to This Popular Sauce,
All Brands Are Not Created Equal." *Boston Herald,* April 25, 2001.

Dyer, Ceil.
Ceil Dyer's Wok Cookery. Tucson, AZ: H.P. Books, 1977.

Goodman Fielder Food Services.
"Your Guide to Better Deep Frying." World Wide Web,
accessed February 20, 2001, at http://www.gffoodservice.com.au.

Han, Chung Hea.
Traditional Korean Cooking. Seoul, Korea:
Chung Woo Publishing Co., 1986.

Healthnotes. "Fats and Oils." World Wide Web, accessed February 10,
2001, at http://www.puritan.com/healthnotes/Food/Fats and Oils.htm.

Herbst, Sharon Tyler.
The New Food Lover's Companion. New York: Barron's, 1995.

Huang, Su-Huei.
Chinese Cuisine. Taipei, Taiwan: Wei-Chuan Publishing Co., 1974.

Hyun, Judy.
The Korean Cookbook. Elizabeth, NJ: Hollym International Corp., 1983.

Jaffrey, Madhur.
Madhur Jaffrey's Far Eastern Cookery. New York: Harper & Row, 1989.

Leung, Mai.
The Classic Chinese Cookbook.
New York: Harper's Magazine Press, 1976.

Lo, Eileen Yin-Fei.
Chinese Kitchen. New York: William Morrow and Company, 1999.

Routhier, Nicole.
The Foods of Vietnam. New York: Stewart, Tabori & Chang, 1989.

Simonds, Nina.
Classic Chinese Cuisine. Shelburne, VT: Chapters Publishing, 1994.

Solomon, Charmaine.
The Complete Asian Cookbook. Rutland, VT: Charles E. Tuttle Co., 1992.

Stacey, Jenny.
Steam Cuisine. Willowdale, Ontario: Firefly Books, 1999.

Zee, A.
Swallowing Clouds. New York: Simon and Schuster, 1990.

INDEX

TABLE OF EQUIVALENTS

The exact equivalents in the following tables have
been rounded for convenience.

LIQUID/DRY MEASURES

U.S.	Metric
¼ teaspoon	1.25 milliliters
½ teaspoon	2.5 milliliters
1 teaspoon	5 milliliters
1 tablespoon (3 teaspoons)	15 milliliters
1 fluid ounce (2 tablespoons)	30 milliliters
¼ cup	60 milliliters
⅓ cup	80 milliliters
½ cup	120 milliliters
1 cup	240 milliliters
1 pint (2 cups)	480 milliliters
1 quart (4 cups, 32 ounces)	960 milliliters
1 gallon (4 quarts)	3.84 liters
1 ounce (by weight)	28 grams
1 pound	454 grams
2.2 pounds	1 kilogram

LENGTH

U.S.	Metric
⅛ inch	3 millimeters
¼ inch	6 millimeters
½ inch	12 millimeters
1 inch	2.5 centimeters

OVEN TEMPERATURE

Fahrenheit	Celsius	Gas
250	120	½
275	140	1
300	150	2
325	160	3
350	180	4
375	190	5
400	200	6
425	220	7
450	230	8
475	240	9
500	260	10